Digital Media, Cultural Production and Speculative Capitalism

This collection of essays explores the interfaces between new information technologies and their impact on contemporary culture, and recent transformations in capitalist production. From a transnational frame, the essays investigate some of the key facets of contemporary global capitalism: the ascendance of finance capital and the increasing importance of immaterial labour (understood here as a post-Fordist notion of work that privileges the art of communication, affect, and virtuosity). The contributors address these transformations by exploring their relation to new digital media (You-Tube, MySpace, digital image and video technology, information networks, etc.) and various cultural forms including the Hispanic television talk show, indigenous video production, documentary film in Southern California, the Latin American stock market, German security surveillance, transnational videoconferencing, and Japanese tourists' use of visual images on cell phones. The authors argue that the seemingly radical newness and alleged immateriality of contemporary speculative capitalism, turns out to be less dramatically new and more grounded in colonial/racial histories of both material and immaterial exploitation than one might at first imagine. Similarly, human interaction with digital media and virtuality, ostensibly a double marker for the contemporary and economically privileged subject, in fact reveals itself in many cases as transgressive of racial, economic and historical categories. This book was published as a special issue of *Social Identities*.

Freya Schiwy is Associate Professor at the University of California, Riverside. She teaches in the Media and Cultural Studies and in the Hispanic Studies Departments. Her current book project is titled "Broadcasting Dissent. Community Media, Latin America, and the Politics of Aesthetics."

Alessandro Fornazzari is an Assistant Professor in the Department of Hispanic Studies at the University of California, Riverside. His area of specialisation is contemporary Latin American literature and culture, and recent research explores the intersections of culture and the economic text in the context of the Latin American neoliberal transitions.

Susan Antebi is Assistant Professor in the Department of Spanish and Portuguese at the University of Toronto. She works in the areas of contemporary Latin American cultural production and disability studies. Her current book project explores interfaces between eugenics and narrative aesthetics in twentieth century Mexico.

Digital Media, Cultural Production and Speculative Capitalism

Edited by
Freya Schiwy, Alessandro Fornazzari and Susan Antebi

Routledge
Taylor & Francis Group

LONDON AND NEW YORK

First published 2011
by Routledge
2 Park Square, Milton Park, Abingdon, Oxon, OX14 4RN

Simultaneously published in the USA and Canada
by Routledge
711 Third Avenue, New York, NY 10017

Routledge is an imprint of the Taylor & Francis Group, an informa business

This book is a reproduction of **Social Identities 15.3**. The Publisher requests to those authors who may be citing this book to state, also, the bibliographical details of the special issue on which the book was based

Typeset in Times New Roman by Taylor & Francis Books.

British Library Cataloguing in Publication Data
A catalogue record for this book is available from the British Library

ISBN13: 978-0-415-61449-8

Disclaimer
The publisher would like to make readers aware that the chapters in this book are referred to as articles as they had been in the special issue. The publisher accepts responsibility for any inconsistencies that may have arisen in the course of preparing this volume for print.

Contents

INTRODUCTION

Digital media, cultural production and speculative capitalism

This collection of essays explores the interfaces between new information technologies, their impact on contemporary culture, and recent transformations in capitalist production. From a transnational frame, the essays investigate some of the key facets of contemporary global capitalism: the relativization of a production based model of capital, the ascendance of finance capital, and the increasing importance of immaterial labor (understood here as a post-Fordist notion of work that privileges the art of communication, affect, and virtuosity). The contributors address these transformations by exploring their relation to new digital media (YouTube, MySpace, digital image and video technology, information networks, etc.) and various cultural forms including the Hispanic television talk show, indigenous video production, documentary film in Southern California, the Latin American stock market, German security surveillance, transnational videoconferencing, and Japanese tourists' use of visual images on cell phones. These diverse analyses of cultural production and digital media – itself a paradigmatic technology of global capitalism – reveal persistent lines of continuity between the virtual and the material, as well as between contemporary and earlier cultures and economies (racial, colonial and imperial legacies). Engaging with recent critical debates on the intrinsic entanglement of the digital and the corporeal and its relation to the logic of global capitalism, the essays collected here offer profoundly transnational perspectives on how we can think about the possibilities for socio-cultural transformation in light of speculative capitalism and the new information and communication technologies.

The essays are the outcome of two years of intense collective debate. Our conversations began in the fall of 2005 in an interdisciplinary and post-area studies faculty research group sponsored by the University of California Riverside's Center for Ideas and Society. At the Center, six of the contributors came together to exchange perspectives on the impact and articulation of digital technologies and speculative capitalism in different contexts: Latin America, Japan, and the USA. Theoretically this conversation brought together the Autonomia perspective on the changing face of capitalism (Mario Tronti, Mauricio Lazzarrato, and Antonio Negri among others) with recent scholarship on digital media (Mark Poster, Katherine Hayles, and Mark Hansen).

Autonomia thinkers have emphasized a historically specific rise of immaterial labor with respect to other forms of labor that corresponds to the current global capitalist economy. This shift, which in the broadest terms corresponds to the passage from secondary (industrialization) to tertiary (informatization) capitalist accumulation, puts the focus on the productive potential of immaterial labor qualities such as flexibility, creativity, innovation, knowledge, communication, and affect. A question that arises from immaterial labor's coming into dominance is whether it undermines anti-capitalist projects that have focused on the production of affect as the ground for the constitution of alternative collective subjectivities. The risk of this structure is complete servitude to a capitalism in which work and intellect, material and immaterial labor, production and consumption have become indistinguishable from one another. Its potential for a politics of liberation seems to lie in a social creativity that transcends class hierarchies, as Mauricio Lazzarrato has written; or, following Paulo Virno's argument, in the radical separation or 'exodus' of intellect from work; or, more recently, in Hardt and Negri's revolutionary subject known as the multitude. These proposals share the view that an outside is no longer possible and that social transformation must be generated and become operative from within.

Digital media scholars, in contrast, have tended to focus their attentions on the specificity of new media forms, such as digital images and electronic hypertexts, and perhaps most importantly, on the interactions of human users and cybernetic machines. If, as Donna Haraway already argued in her now classic cyborg manifesto, the merging of the biological and the mechanical offers radical new possibilities for the disruption of traditional subject categories, this uncertain fusion also points towards the fantasy that material bodies are becoming obsolete – replaced by abstract information that circulates rapidly as code, through interchangeable, and ultimately disposable hardware platforms. Countering this fantasy, scholarship by Hayles and Hansen, among others, has emphasized the persistence of materiality in contemporary media, arguing in some cases that the digital is in fact intimately dependent upon embodied experience, and in this sense, intensely corporeal.

Despite obvious disparities between these two traditions, we were intrigued by their points of contact, and the problems these sometimes posed. The notion of immaterial labor as a labor that produces no durable or material good (such as a service, knowledge, or communication) also appears to be reflected in the fear – or fantasy – that the rise of digital technology means the disappearance of substance behind the code, or of a grounded referent behind the image. Media scholars' insistence on the materiality of the digital complicates this parallel, although in many cases an emphasis on material specificity does not necessarily translate into leverage through which to postulate socio-political or cultural transformation, but remains instead at the level of a global capitalist self-reproducing and digitally networked system.

In conjunction with these debates, consideration of the ongoing colonial legacy of global capitalism allowed us to further complicate our understanding of the roles of new technologies in contemporary economies. Specifically, the immaterial qualities of colonialist discourse and their racial and gender imaginaries have long been fundamental to global capitalist expansion, and indeed have constituted the basis of its operations. In this sense, the seemingly radical newness – and alleged immateriality – of contemporary speculative capitalism, turns out to be less dramatically new and more grounded in histories of both material and immaterial exploitation than one might at first imagine. Similarly, human interaction with digital media and virtuality, ostensibly a double marker for the contemporary and economically privileged subject, in fact reveals itself in many cases as transcendent and transgressive of racial, economic and historical categories. This is the case, for example, when Andean indigenous communities create and distribute their own digital videos, or when nineteenth century colonialist entertainment forms such as ethnographic spectacles turn out to run on circuits powered by a blend of laboring bodies and collectively accepted codes of authenticity and ethnic difference.

Working from the interstices of these traditions a project emerged that situates new digital technologies in a broader global economic order and stresses the relevance of keeping colonial and modern lines of continuity in sight as we grapple with the speed and depth of socio-cultural transformations occasioned by new technologies.

This collective project was further developed and refined in the intense workshop atmosphere of a three-day panel at the annual meeting of the American Comparative Literature Association in the Spring of 2007 in Puebla, Mexico. The contributors' research papers were placed in dialogue with other transnational perspectives on digital media and global capitalism, and our thinking gained further depth. The collection presented here for publication includes some of these additional papers and maintains our radically post-area studies perspective, taking advantage of our different local positions in order to work towards a globally informed theorization of new information technology and speculative capitalism.

Antebi and Schiwy open up the collection of essays with two contributions that highlight continuities between the virtual and material. In 'The Talk Show Uploaded: YouTube and the Technicity of the Body,' Antebi explores the corporeal continuities manifest in what is often thought as a disembodied form of representation, namely, the television talk show and its contemporary recirculation on YouTube. Her essay traces historical links between the freak show and the television talk show, specifically emphasizing the nationalistic anxiety present in both virtual and material encounters between Latin American and Latino/a talk show viewers and participants. YouTube allows users to highlight specific program episodes, and to integrate them with personal commentary. Antebi argues that this instant and virtual reappropriation of 'trash TV' goes beyond the dilemma of authenticity and fraudulence that so consistently haunts both the freak show and its talk show successors, instead refocusing viewer attention towards the 'empty husk' (Hansen) of the corporeal, national image. Yet rather than suggesting the abandonment of corporeal presence in television and internet entertainment, this 'husk' itself becomes the object of enjoyment, and allows the viewer to reconsider the geopolitics of circulating body images, from transnational talk shows to their freak show legacy.

Schiwy's 'Digital Ghosts, Global Capitalism, and Social Change' traces the importance of colonial legacies for theorizing speculative capitalism by thinking from the use of digital media by indigenous social movements in the Andes. She argues that the racialized body remains tangible as digital media are read and used akin to older, analogue technology and its 'writing of light.' The desires for truth and corporeality in indigenous media point to the existence of borders from which alternatives to the current capitalist order are imagined and enacted. Similarly then, in indigenous films speculative capitalism betrays its colonial constitution that ties it back to modern/colonial economic forms, rather than creating an entirely novel break with the past.

Rogers and Fornazzari focus on the implications of contemporary critical art for understanding the nature of speculative capitalism. In 'The Aesthetics of Implication: Toward the Functional Axis of Labor Politics in Contemporary Art and Media,' Rogers analyzes an experimental documentary collaboration between Juan Devis and Yoshua Okón. This film works through the politics of immigrant day-laboring in southern California, in order to examine how a new global and economic order comprised of supranational trade agreements (particularly NAFTA), new forms of communication and information technologies, modes of immaterial and 'affective' labor (Michael Hardt), and transnational economic flows have elicited an alternative form of anti-capitalist critique in art and culture. Rogers argues that this critique no longer represents the inequities of labor but rather deliberately implicates itself in the social and economic systems it seeks to undermine. The documentary approaches what Rogers calls 'the functional axis of labor' – the infolding of systems and procedures in and around the work that reveals the deep structural inequities of global labor practice by reflexively co-implicating themselves, their film, and ultimately the viewer into the labor of the film's production – demonstrating how the work's exchange value is dependent upon the surplus labor of others.

Fornazzari's 'A Stock Market Theory of Value' engages the problem of neoliberal dedifferentiation by focusing on Latin American representations of what Pierre-Joseph Proudhon called 'the monument *par excellence* of modern society': the stock market. In the context of the Southern Cone neoliberal transitions, the stock market's logic of second order abstraction is shown to reveal some of the profound transformations put into effect by finance capitalism's focus on the money form (the anachronistic state of productivist centered political economy, high risk speculation, and the electronic free flow of finance and information). Focusing on the 1980s Chilean stock market boom and the fin de siècle Argentinean economic crisis, this paper explores the stock market theory of value that emerges out of the so-called new economic paradigm based on information technology.

Mejía, Kim and Foster explore different uses of new media and what these uses imply for the notion of referentiality so dear to modernity, industrial capitalism, and analogue technology now called into question with the proliferation of representation based on digital codes. Mejía's article explores the use of new technologies by Ecuadorian migrants to the US and Europe who find themselves negotiating the reality they physically inhabit and the responsibilities and commitments that bind them to Ecuador. She maintains that, transformed by the irruption of new technologies intent upon shrinking space and time, nostalgia is becoming 'digital.' Digital nostalgia, then, is about the quest for continuity of space and time through the simultaneity offered by digital media.

Kim's 'Südlandia: Referentiality in Foucault, Security Cameras in Germany' reexamines the question of referentiality in Michel Foucault's Archeology of Knowledge through the German cultural signifier 'südländisch.' He argues that the relation between referent and discourse in Foucault should be understood in terms of how 'südländisch' circulates as a free floating signifier: it generates the appearance of reference yet without a referent. 'Südländisch' is an untranslatable adjective in German, 'literally' meaning 'southern' but indexing its enunciator's desires and fears. Its associations include warmth, sex, the color brown, as well as crime, filth and 'foreigners' who are imagined to stem from the Mediterranean. Focusing on an attempted 'terrorist' bombing plot in Summer 2006 in Germany, Kim discusses a fuzzy security camera image of a terrorist suspect described by police and the news media as appearing 'südländisch.' He maintains that the referential is that which has all of the appearance of a 'referent' but is rather a topos upon which discourse gathers and on which vision is trained. Hence, the question of referentiality in Foucault hitherto posed by critics and cynics has been wrongly configured. The true question should be, 'How does discourse create the appearance of reference?'

Foster's contribution, 'Tourism and the Digital Gaze: What Time is this Picture?,' concludes this collection. It considers how cell phone cameras are altering Japanese domestic tourism. At crowded festivals, tourists hold phones above the heads of other spectators to capture an otherwise unseeable sight. They transmit images to friends as immediate personalized postcards. Moments after an event, they scroll through their pictures, nostalgic for moments just past. The cell phone as a medium for visual production and consumption radically changes the way memories are encoded and communicated, instantaneously transforming the boundless tourist experience into a bounded visual text that can be manipulated, sent, and, ultimately, deleted. While Japanese-made camera phones are a vital part of the global electronics market, their ubiquity within Japan has reshaped the tourist landscape, making traditional distinctions between authentic/inauthentic, real/representation, here/there increasingly irrelevant.

The essays collected unravel the question of what changes and what remains in the transition to a global speculative economy relying on digital media and technology from different disciplinary perspectives in the humanities. Rather than focusing exclusively on the purported novelty of contemporary global capitalism and the digital technologies that frequently accompany it, we have sought to unpack both economic and technological histories as well as their points of intersection, in order to reconsider our understanding of the contemporary fascination with the immaterial, the digital, and the virtual. By looking more closely at the circulation of these concepts, as well as the specific technologies behind them, we have been able to sharpen our definitions of how and when new technologies have emerged in interaction with a global economy, and in what sense the cultural meanings of these technologies demands a rereading of the histories from which they have become inseparable. In addition, specific attention in several of these essays to paradigmatic transitional moments in economic history allows the collection as a whole to reflect upon the nature of contemporary global capitalism, as refracted through artistic and political expression, and to open a space for thinking through possibilities – and limitations – of radical transformation and critique.

One of the more significant theoretical challenges for this group of essays as a whole has been our collective negotiation of the problem of assumed disembodiment – in digital media images, for example – in opposition to the notion of a lingering or constitutive materiality. If referentiality is seen in some cases as a modern desire, now left behind by increasingly disembodied media forms, new media continues to call forth desires for and interrogations of materiality, perhaps as a lingering specter of earlier economies and cultural production, or in fact as the irrevocable underpinning of digitality, whose projected disembodiment belies an ongoing corporeal anchor. Does the desire for and reflection upon materiality in the midst of twenty-first century constellations of digital technology and speculative capitalism function as a backwards glance towards globalization's colonial legacy? Or does the apparent contemporary virtuality of economics, cultural production and life forms rather point towards earlier versions of immaterial circulation that we now begin to recognize as such? Taken together, our essays suggest that both operations may be at work, and that the transhistorical, transmaterial exchange of glances will become crucial to understanding, negotiating and reshaping the historical legacies of global capitalism.

Freya Schiwy
Media and Cultural Studies Department, University of California, Riverside

Susan Antebi
Department of Hispanic Studies, University of California, Riverside

Alessandro Fornazzari
Department of Hispanic Studies, University of California Riverside

The talk show uploaded: YouTube and the technicity of the body

Susan Antebi

Department of Hispanic Studies, University of California, Riverside, USA

The dramatic success of YouTube and related internet sites in recent years has led to a shift in public interaction with many television programs, including popular and controversial television talk shows, such as Peruvian Laura Bozzo's *Laura en América*. While television talk shows and other media have long participated in the production and circulation of racial, national, and class-based stereotyped images, the interplay between television, YouTube and independent internet use allows for new modes of engagement between embodied subjects and digital images. Through analysis of uploaded clips of Laura Bozzo's show, homemade videos and user commentary, this article addresses changes and continuities in the structure of interpellation, through which identities circulate via popular Spanish language internet media. Building upon recent work by Mark Hansen regarding corporeal technicity, the article suggests that contemporary internet use blurs the contours of the stereotyped media image, and harnesses the user into a complex dynamic of both virtual and embodied identity delineation.

In June 2007, an incendiary rumor, fueled by a set of video postings, began to circulate on the international Peruvian community blogosphere. The rumor focussed on talk show celebrity Laura Bozzo, and on the ethics and legality of both her show and her publicity activities. The fact that Bozzo continues to inspire angry critique and gossip is hardly surprising, given the success of her shows, and the history of scandal surrounding her, from public disgust with her portrayal of poor Peruvians, to charges of her involvement in political corruption.[1]

In this 2007 case, critique of Bozzo stemmed specifically from the work of bloggers, who juxtaposed two videos, one from Bozzo's talk show, featuring a young girl from Lima, allegedly the victim of sexual abuse, and the second from a video of Bozzo's visit to Pisco, following the earthquake that left many surviving residents homeless. In the Pisco video, a young girl cries as she tells Laura of her predicament following the earthquake, just as the girl on Bozzo's show had cried as she told how she was afraid of her step-father. Could the two girls actually be one and the same? Some bloggers insisted that the girl who appeared in both videos was a paid actress. The news program *Prensa Libre* used information from blogs in a report affirming that the girl in the Pisco video was the same girl who appeared on Bozzo's show. As anchorwoman Rosa María Palacios states: 'No estamos cien por ciento seguros de que sea la misma niña pero hemos visto el video muchas veces y estamos casi seguros de que se trata de la misma criatura' [We are not one hundred percent sure that it's the same girl, but we've seen the video many times and we're almost certain that it is the same child]. A YouTube video posted in November of the same year includes the *Prensa Libre* report, followed by a clip from *Magaly te ve* (a program on celebrity gossip) with discussion of the same story (sheenny, 8 November 2007).

Accounts of the falsification of stories on television talk shows are so common as to be considered by many to be a normal part of the industry. In this case, however, the mode of circulation and production of the story is somewhat unusual. Rather than an instance of bloggers commenting on a news item, here, a news program constructs its version of events based on a blog-generated montage of video clips. The YouTube synthesis of the story is merely one more element in a chain of media representation, in which cause and effect, as well as anecdote and commentary, blur into one another, making the origin of the scandal difficult to pinpoint. Similarly, the faces of the girls in the two videos (or the face of the one girl) blur together and apart. Watching these clips, we may wonder if it will ever be possible to decide if it's the same person in both, and if, in fact, it makes any difference. The girl on the screen is undoubtedly young, poor and mestiza, or possibly indigenous. In this sense, many Peruvian viewers might conceivably identify with her, at least to some degree. Still, the ongoing undecidability of the identity(ies) of the girl(s) continues to haunt the images, coupled with the sense that this is probably one girl portrayed in two different scenes. How, then, might such images – as well as their dual charge of insistence and uncertainty – participate in the production and circulation of identities, in relation to the familiar categories of nation, race and class?

In this essay I read the question of digitally mediated embodiment through attention to the relatively recent phenomenon of YouTube videos. I consider the segments of television talk shows by Laura Bozzo that viewers splice and upload to the internet, interspersing them with homemade videos and commentary. In reading this contemporary genre and use of the television talk show, I look at the construction and interpellation of race, nation and class through body images – such as those from the videos described above – as modes through which identities circulate and produce – or fail to produce – meaning.

While the generalized scenario of interpellation may sound familiar, attention to the specificity of digital media in this case allows the viewer, or the critic, to reconsider the process. If, according to a classic Butlerian reading, the emergence of a subject and the subject's agency are irrevocably bound into an initiating moment of interpellation by external authority or normativity, recent work by Mark Hansen asks us to approach the question via the framework of what he terms 'mixed reality.' In mixed reality, as Hansen writes, 'coupling with the domain of social images occurs *from within the operational perspective* of the organism and thus comprises a component of its primordial embodied agency' (2006, p. 13). The notion of mixed reality is based on a rereading of interactions between embodied subjects and so-called virtual (digitized) reality, so that the virtual is dependent upon and intertwined with embodied perception. Rather than seeing virtual reality as a separate realm of representations outside the body, in this case the body continues to act upon and to determine the contours of its mixed reality world. In the two videos discussed above, for example, one might imagine how viewers' experience and interpretation of what they observe on the screen blend into the virtual body(ies) depicted in each clip, particularly when interpretation includes the acts of online commentary, video juxtaposition, and repeated mouse-clicking and viewing. At the same time, the impossibility of proving that the two girls are actually one, combined with bloggers' angry insistence that this is the case, effectively empties the contents of the images themselves, since what stands out is the resemblance between the two. Each image points to the other, and intersects with the viewer's perceptions, in a three-way circuit that blurs the contours of conventional interpellation.

The scenario initiated by these juxtaposed videos and their rapid circulation on the internet and on television is of course part of the broader phenomenon of proliferating digital entertainment technologies over the past decade. Large-scale public use of these technologies in turn forms a backdrop to academic and popular fascination with the shifting roles of human bodies as they intersect and overlap with virtual realms of cyberspace and with the more specific parameters of digital code. Critical debates on the materiality of the body, in tension with notions of disembodied information have become familiar to readers of the work of N. Katherine Hayles, Vivian Sobchack and Mark Hansen, among others, and suggest that corporeality can now scarcely be approached or considered without reference to digital media. The encounter between the body and such media in some instances reduces to the dilemma of a contest. Will the material specificity of the body prevail, or be abstracted into code and thus somehow lost? As Hayles eloquently showed in her *How we became posthuman,* and in her more recent *My mother was a computer,* the actual loss of the body is more a science fiction fantasy than an accurate reading of new media and artificial intelligence (2005, p. 2). The digital code that allows media and its virtual realms to operate remains persistently material, and in many cases intertwined with the human body, as Mark Hansen also suggests in his *New philosophy for new media*: 'If the digital image foregrounds the processural framing of data by the body, what it ultimately yields is less a framed object than an embodied, subjective experience that can only be felt' (2003, p. 13). Throughout his more recent work, *Bodies in code*, Hansen continues to emphasize a reading of digital media grounded in affectivity and lived embodiment. According to this reading, the body is always already immersed in technics, hence exterior to itself, and in this sense potentially freed from the double bind of embodied agency and interpellation.

In the case of the talk show, and in the YouTube circulation of talk show segments, racialized and extreme body images continue to proliferate, producing opportunities for identification and differentiation amongst studio and television audience members, hence potentially interpellating nationally or regionally specific public sectors. Yet given the shifts in format, from a history of live spectacle, to television, to the rapid, digitized circulation of clips, allowing the public to create, select and comment – as individuals – upon sequenced images, what, effectively, remains of interpellation and materially embedded subject agency? Or in other words, how might Hansen's notion of the mixed reality that marks interactions and continuities between embodied agency and digital media affect the production and circulation of identities in these videos? According to a mixed reality approach, YouTube videos and their images are not external representations that interrogate their users, but are instead bound inseparably into users' lived experience and embodied agency. Does this particular form of new media then allow users and viewers to move beyond the classic conundrum of racialized interpellation that is said to structure earlier modes of entertainment such as freak shows and ethnographic spectacles? And how might this media allow us to better understand embodied agency in both talk shows and internet activity? These are questions I consider in my approach to the phenomenon of Laura Bozzo on YouTube, focusing both on the specificity of the medium of the spectacle in question, and on elements of theoretical continuity between talk shows and YouTube circulation.

The repeating return to the question of the body, as part of an overarching dilemma of subjectivity and agency, suggests a kind of self-reflexive embarrassment, or shame, with which the body is frequently associated, both in scholarship and in corporeal spectacle, of the kind featured on Laura Bozzo's show, for example. As Žižek describes in a Lacanian reading of ethics, violence and subjectivity, shame is associated with the uncertain nexus between body and phantasmatic nucleus, or in other words between the apparent passivity of the body and the subject's intimate experience of enjoyment. 'En síntesis, "vergüenza" designa el hecho de que el espíritu esté directamente vinculado con una realidad corporal inerte y vulgar' (Žižek, 2005, p. 85) [In synthesis, 'shame' designates the fact that 'spirit' is directly tied to an inert and vulgar corporeal reality]. The structure Žižek proposes resonates effectively when brought to bear on the problem of the body as theoretical object. The shame of the body, whether experienced intimately, or posed as an abstract conundrum, is thus not related so much to the body as such, but more specifically to unresolved problems of contextualization. Writing in 1993, Judith Butler described a feeling of naïveté, when asked, in response to her work on the performativity of gender, 'what about the materiality of the body, Judy?' (Butler, 1993, p. 3) as if the question exposed her uncomfortably, as an embodied subject behind the theory, and indeed, literally infantilized her through use of an informal diminutive version of her name. In contrast, critical work on the body since the mid-1990s has tended to insist so much on the constructed nature of the body, that reference to material, 'real' or extratextual bodies may run the risk of coming across as embarrassingly naïve (Hansen, 2006, p. 7). Tobin Siebers points towards a similar dilemma when he writes: 'It is a prejudice of literary studies to assert either that the complexity of texts is greater than that of nontextual objects or that nontextual objects simply do not exist' (2004, p. 1323, n. 1). The corporeal embarrassment – or shame – reflected in each of these cases, operates at the crossover point between an object and its so-called context, or at the point of disjuncture between seemingly incompatible ideas. In this sense, the notion of embarrassment becomes inseparable from a reading of corporeal technicity. This structure of embarrassment is useful to my reading of spectacle here, because in the talk show and related genres as well, a similar kind of embarrassment is central to the audience's enjoyment, and to ambivalences between belief and disbelief, and between identification/interpellation and the collective blurring of identity categories. In the case of YouTube, the emergence of embarrassment stems from moments of realization that the dividing line between audience and spectacle has suddenly broken down, that the processes of viewing, reacting to and interacting with the show are both as private as one's living room and as public as the internet, that digital interactivity is a lived embodied experience, that the message that seems to have been sent directly to me was in fact intended for everyone, and no one (or vice versa); and perhaps, that what seemed to be for free has an unknown kind of price tag. And we may realize, in repeatedly viewing the two juxtaposed Bozzo videos of the victimized child(ren), discussed above, that our own insistence on repeating these clips, one after the other, has become inseparable from the embodiment of one girl digitized as two.

YouTube was launched in 2005 and has already achieved immense success and international popularity, but has also been at the center of legal battles regarding copyright law, as network television has struggled to defend its market, even while certain programs and marketing groups benefit from free increased exposure.[2] In this sense, YouTube exemplifies the uncertainty of the explosion of digital entertainment media, caught between paradigms of monolithic and more dispersed market control. The division is most clearly visible in the details of the operations that transpose television programs to a YouTube format. Although users are limited to video postings of ten minutes in length, many bypass the restriction by simply dividing longer clips into ten minute segments. Users also frequently display an irreverent urge to mine programs for their content; disregarding the television networks' slick image quality control, a few seem to take digital film of a television screen while the program is running, sometimes adding their own voiceovers. Such techniques demonstrate the ragged quality of the divide between formats, where rapid circulation and re-interpretation remain partially embedded in the trappings of standard television programming, which in turn start to become part of a vast system of uploading and dissemination.

This phenomenon underscores the uncertain and blurred quality of the shift between media forms, and suggests that the new and freer circulation of the YouTube model continues to be marked with the seemingly more tangible weight of its television precursor. In a similar sense, the sequence of YouTube videos featuring or discussing Laura Bozzo and her cultural impact are weighed down by hotly debated dilemmas of ethnic and national identity. Thus, if the digital entertainment model seemed to promise a realm in which materially embodied identities are left behind, and users circulate as virtual versions of the temporary selves they choose, the YouTube space in particular shows that embodied, nationally specific identities are at least as significant as they were on conventional television. What remains to be determined here, however, are the ways in which these identities continue to emerge and circulate, and how the relatively new YouTube format might work, in conjunction with the history of talk shows and related spectacles, to impact this process.

Perhaps the most pressing issue for YouTube users who participate in the video montages and debates on Laura Bozzo is the image of Perú and of Peruvians in international context. The most consistent critique of Bozzo rests on the supposedly negative image of Peruvians that her show constructs and makes available to pan-Hispanic audiences, particularly as the show was originally distributed through the Miami-based network, Telemundo, and is now available through cable channels and pay-per-view. Homemade videos include clips of Peruvians who bemoan the public image Bozzo has created for them. One participant notes, for example, that friends who learn she is Peruvian are surprised that she has teeth (Callevip, 2007). This example undoubtedly points to one element of the intertwined discourses of race and class that the show, and YouTube reactions, make evident, as well as to the feelings of personal embarrassment that the show implies for Peruvians living abroad. While Laura Bozzo herself appears as relatively tall, blonde, with stereotypically European facial features, and carefully groomed, most of the participants on her show tend to be shorter, darker in skin tone, apparently of Peruvian mestizo background, and often, as in the case above, without clear evidence of access to dental care. Regardless of the racial, ethnic and socio-economic categories with which Laura Bozzo and these participants might actually identify, the visual spectacle of the show sets up a clear contrast between Bozzo and her participants, as well as those who make up the studio audience. In addition, Bozzo's highly visible activities in fund-raising and advocacy for marginalized Peruvians, particularly women and children, habilitates and makes public an explicit, racially marked divide between wealthier and poorer Peruvians, as exemplified in the video, 'Laura Bozzo La gran ayudadora' (Provincia, 2007). Unlike the experience of simply watching Bozzo's television show itself, browsing through YouTube clips and home-made montages about Laura allows a densely charged landscape of racial and class based national divisions to emerge, as participants and viewers contribute and comment on the video segments, and on one another.

Bozzo's televised appearances of her recent visit to Pisco, Perú, following the disastrous earthquake that left many in the town dead and others without homes or access to basic necessities including water and health care, further underscored fraught separations between racial and socio-economic groups in Perú, as well as the media's role in making visible such categories. In one YouTube clip, a different television hostess (Magaly Medina) attacks Bozzo for her exploitation of Pisco as media opportunity, and includes footage of Bozzo in dialogue with earthquake victims (Powerpollito, 2007).

Many users and respondents on the YouTube site are also particularly offended by the behavior of the show's participants, and viewers comments suggest that such behavior is seen as part and parcel of the negative, racialized images that Bozzo generates. As is well known to viewers of this variety of daytime television talk show, common practices include physical fights between participants. For this reason, professional staff are always on hand to break up the violence and prevent excessive bodily harm. The most classic scenario involves the revelation of marital infidelity or similar behavior, followed by the spontaneous fighting of the parties involved. There is also a televised interview of Bozzo by Peruvian writer and television host Jaime Bayly who insists on the problem of the violence represented on Bozzo's show, and suggests that such scenes make all Peruvians look bad, while improving Laura's ratings. Laura, for her part, insists that her show offers women the only space in which they can legitimately and safely hit men, usually their husbands or boyfriends, who undoubtedly deserve to be beaten for what they have done. She also emphasizes here that absolutely everything presented on the show is real (Ndigital, 2007). The apparent continuity between morality and truth upheld in this dialogue is not incidental, and points to a recurring, self-representing discourse of such shows' positive social role.

Insistence on the issue of truth, and on the possibility of verifiable authenticity, turn out to be hallmarks of the television talk show in general, which in turn link the genre to its freak show precursor. Yet the verification of the truth in such programming, and in YouTube commentary, also corresponds to Umberto Eco's 1983 definition of 'Neo TV,' in contrast to 'Paleo TV.' Neo TV, according to Eco in his classic analysis of Italian television in the early 1980s, tends to focus on itself and its contact with the public, rather than on external referents in the world (Eco, 1983, p. 246). As Claudia Laudano describes with respect to Eco in her discussion of television talk shows in the 1990s, in Neo TV, the truth of the act of making a statement replaces the truth of the statement as such. This newer truth is constructed through intersubjective networks between television performers and viewers, and depends upon the constant revelation of evidence of live television production: cameras, lights, microphones and technical personnel (Laudano, 1998, p. 34).

As in the case of the television programs referenced by Eco, and by Laudano, Laura Bozzo's program clearly participates in the ongoing paradigm of Neo TV. A classic example is Laura's persistent refrain, 'un aplauso,' upon which the studio audience always bursts into applause. As Eco notes, this standard technique of Neo TV establishes a marked contrast to the canned laughter or applause format of shows featured on Paleo TV. According to Eco, the viewer of Neo TV appreciates the use of applause on command, since it affirms the televisual truth of the camera as witness to coded interaction between the show's host and the studio audience (p. 250). In this sense, the applause is real in a way that the secretly prompted applause of Paleo TV never could be. Laura also employs the technique of revealing televisual equipment, by incorporating one of her cameramen into the show through occasional verbal exchanges, thus upholding Eco's reading of Neo TV's discourse, and disguising the fact that another, unseen camera must necessarily be filming the scenes. Contemporary use of YouTube to re-broadcast TV clips takes the Neo TV paradigm a step further; the authenticity of each clip, or montage, is upheld by the additional framing of the YouTube format itself; the upload itself becomes the undeniable, self-referential fact of internet truth.

Bozzo's insistence that everything represented on her show is real functions as an echo of the kinds of truth claims made by P.T. Barnum and his colleagues in the heyday of the freak show, in which exaggerated claims and outright deception became part of the structure of the spectacle.[3] Studies of the talk show, such as Josh Gamson's *Freaks talk back*, in fact suggest that dishonesty is consistently built into the production of such shows, as in cases where individuals are paid to perform roles, 'as themselves,' while being encouraged to highlight a particular angle of a story (Gamson, 1998, p. 81; Tolson, 2001, pp. 1–30). And episodes of Laura's show demonstrate that the construction of scenarios built around the progressive revelation of the 'true version' of a story frequently provide the program's primary entertainment value. Regardless of what viewers and participants actually believe in the final analysis, enjoyment, as well as spectacles of suffering, are consistently derived from surprising contrasts between different versions of a given story. It is also interesting to note that the 'proof' of what allegedly took place is typically confirmed through resources such as hidden (or not so hidden) cameras showing scenes of marital infidelity, even when the supposed culprit might insist that the person featured on the screen is in fact someone else. In this sense, final proofs depend less on juridically derived notions of material evidence, and more on the stylized repetition of talk show discourse and its media, in this case, the self-revealing hidden camera. In the era of internet access to talk show clips, the discourse of truth depends on the possibility of unlimited repetition and circulation. The more often a clip is reproduced and played, the more it affirms that it is identical to itself, hence digitally coded as true.

In examining YouTube sequences from and about Laura Bozzo's show, I want to emphasize what is innovative in this medium and its circulation of racial and national identities, but at the same time, how these examples serve as a window onto both recent and distant histories of corporeal spectacle. Many of the available sequences simply reproduce episodes from Laura's show, whether from her 'Laura en América' (later called simply, 'Laura') or the more recent 'Laura sin censura,' which replaced it on cable channels and pay-per-view, some time after Telemundo cancelled the original program. Since users can continuously upload new segments as they choose, the format offers viewers a steady diet of Laura selections of about 10 minutes in length, whenever they wish to sample them, as well as the opportunity to form on-line communities through comments and dialogue. YouTube bypasses the problem of access to cable and pay-per-view in this case, because anyone with an internet connection can watch the selections, free of additional charges, and participate instantly in online conversations about them. Thus, if the scandalous nature of Laura's work led to Telemundo's cancellation of the show, making it less accessible and more expensive, the same tendency, fortuitously coupled with the rise of YouTube, at once has allowed the program to circulate more rapidly and freely than ever before.

Some of the available sequences are explicit in their treatment of race and nationality, as is the case in a four-part segment with the title 'Cholo soy, y no me compadezcas' [I am a *cholo* and don't feel sorry for me] (daniperu25, 19 October 2007). Here, the premise is that in two separate cases, mothers are distressed that their daughters are involved with men of highland indigenous background. The mothers and daughters also claim to be of mixed racial background, Afro-Peruvian in one case, mestizo in the second, so that tension accrues around divisions between coastal and highland ethnic identities, as well as between 'lighter' and 'darker' populations. This episode is hardly a bold attack on racism in Perú, since both of the mothers are made to look so extreme and ridiculous in their views that one is forced to wonder if they could possibly be expressing their own beliefs. Laura is direct in her criticism of their unabashed racism, and the studio audience backs her up with applause for the *cholos,* and jeers at all expressions of racism. Another participant on the show, a lighter-skinned man who claims to be Italian and is interested in one of the young women, also receives boos from the audience, especially when they learn that he is actually a Peruvian who pretends to be of various different nationalities in order to seduce women. The sequence functions alternately as a farce, and as an entertaining celebration of Peruvian racial and national identity, concluding with the interpretation of the song 'Cholo soy y no me compadezcas' by the special guest singer Luis Abanto Morales.

Part of the irony of this episode's apparent anti-racism lies in the fact that the category *cholo*, though at one time considered insulting, has been widely redefined as a popular marker of national ethnic identity, so that Peruvians of a broad range of backgrounds and skin-tones can claim it with pride. In this sense, the *cholo* figure oscillates easily between victim of marked racial discrimination, and overarching national icon. Coming to the *cholo*'s defense is hardly a risky stance to take; failing to do so in this context might imply self-hatred and the rejection of Peruvian national identity. Yet the positions taken by the allegedly racist participants on the show are so absurd and extreme that it becomes difficult to take race or ethnicity seriously here at all. This is particularly the case in the participation of the 'Italian,' Gino, who arrives on stage wearing dark sunglasses and a large backpack, as he claims he is ready to travel, and indeed to take one of the young women with him to Italy.

The ambiguity and humor of the national and ethnic categories in circulation here make it ridiculous to try to define the actual identities and opinions of the participants, as well as those of the online commentators and studio audience members. When the audience claps along to the popular Huayno track 'Píopío,' and the young women dance with their *cholo* boyfriends, the enjoyment and celebration of Peruvian identity, cultural tradition, and indigenous ethnicity is certainly evident, yet it is equally certain that each of these categories may be heavily framed in quotation marks. This is because the notion of the *cholo* here suggests both a specific physiognomy, especially facial features and skin color, and an open-ended nationalism in which everyone present is impelled to participate. Laura's guests make references to one another's facial features and skin color, for example, suggesting that the mother of one of the young women should look in the mirror before attacking others as *cholo*. And part of the plotline driving the story forward is the revelation of the 'real' identity of Gino, the fake Italian. At the same time, ethnic identities are not clear-cut here; everyone who dances and claps to the Huayno music becomes a *cholo*, at least temporarily, and when Gino turns out to be just another Peruvian (as if there were any doubt), his farcical role as Europeanized counterpoint to the nationalist celebration is revealed for what it is – an effective and entertaining simulation. Of course, the joke implies that any ethnic or national identity, including that of the *cholo*, can be tried on and played with. The contents of these categories is thus perpetually emptied out and resifted; the identities are at once within and beyond the staged bodies that purport to represent them. An intriguing culmination to this staging occurs when the singer, Luis Abanto Morales, comes onto the stage, elegantly dressed in a suit and ready to sing 'Cholo soy y no me compadezcas.' The camera moves briefly here to focus on the face of the first representative *cholo* boyfriend, who appears now to be distinctly displeased. Although it may be impossible to identity the reason for this, one might imagine that at this point, the show's participants find themselves upstaged by the real celebrity, distinguished by his fame, musical talent, clothing, and above all, by his ability to combine these attributes with the convincing embodiment of a *cholo* identity that ostensibly speaks to all Peruvians. The '*cholo soy*' discourse plays with the notions of ethnicity and nationality, but clearly it does not erase socio-economic class boundaries. The crudely overarching and glamorous representation of national, *cholo* identity is of course, entertaining, but somehow also embarrassing, as it marks what it cannot quite include.

A look at the online YouTube reactions to the various segments of this episode further reveals the uncertainty of the national and ethnic categories in question, and the medium-specific processes through which these categories continue to circulate. The segments, as well as many other Laura episodes, were uploaded to YouTube by a user named daniperu25, identified as Daniel, a 26 year-old living in the United States. In the comments following each segment, other users thank 'dani' for making the show available, and dani responds to individual comments, and writes that he will upload another segment after lunch. Discussion focuses on various definitions of the term *cholo*, as well as on the relative stupidity, racism and ugliness of some of the participants. In the spontaneous creation of this online community, users both define and distance themselves vis à vis the categories represented on the show. Communication functions beyond the power dynamics of commercial television production, since in this case, a semi-anonymous dani, rather than Laura, is the center of attention, simply because he serves as the conduit to an externally available broadcast. This role includes the privilege of access to restricted media since, at the time of the uploads, the show was no longer freely available on major network television. Dani gets to decide when each segment will appear, and in what order, thus partially controlling the drama and suspense as a particular story unfolds. At the same time, dani, and the many others who fulfill similar functions on YouTube, operate on a par with users who simply observe and comment on the uploaded episodes. This means that each can make written comments, and choose whether or not to respond to others. And the identity of each is typically defined by a username, age, country of residence, and any other information s/he may wish to give in commentary, meaning that levels of anonymity tend to equalize across this spectrum of YouTube users.

 In this extended dissemination of Laura's show, participants partially replicate the original show's structure, by making comments that may identify them by their opinions as well as by the racial or national identities they claim. The televisual truth of ethnic and national identity shifts towards a YouTube truth, in which everyone claims some degree of critical distance from the television participants, and in which the uncertainty surrounding terms such as *cholo* can be debated by all who wish to log in. Following is a selection of user comments to this episode:

Intimo1901: '(…) en el Peru no somos cholos somos mestizos. Que fea palabra "cholo"' [In Peru we aren't cholos, we are mestizos. What an ugly word, 'cholo']

Intimo1901: 'esa mujer tiene sangre indigena y es racista con su propia gente' [That woman has indigenous blood and she is racist with her own people]

Republicana88: 'cholo? no es ladron? un cholo, un personaje no se' [cholo? Isn't it a thief? A cholo, a character, I don't know]

denisan47: 'perdon pero que significa la palabra "cholo"? me encanta conocer significados de otros paises, alguien me explica esa palabra? Pleaseee …' [Excuse me but what does the word 'cholo' mean? I love to learn the meanings of words from other countries, could someone explain that word to me? Pleasee]

litacrasy: 'cholo quiere decir alguien de la sierra del peru, los que tienen cara asi como de los incas. La mayoria son de cusco y eso cholo = persona de la sierra' [cholo means someone from the highlands of Peru, those who have a face sort of like the incas. Most are from Cusco. Cholo =person from the highlands]

beckerf4n: 'error, cholo viene d chala qu es costa, los costeños somos los cholos, los de las sierra son SERRANOS.' [error, cholo comes from chala which is on the coast, people from the coast, we are cholos, those from the highlands are HIGHLANDERS]

xxxxnancy: 'depende como lo uses. Si es ofensa lo que quieres significa indio serrano inferior. Si es un tono no tan ofensivo es mestizo. Y si es usado como carino le puedes decir cholito a tu hijito o a tu pareja.' [it depends on how you use it. If you want to offend it means inferior highland Indian. If it's a less offensive tone it means mestizo. If it is used with affection you can call your child or your partner *cholito*]

Republicana88: 'pues mi novio es medio costeño y medio serrano y como kieroooo a mi cholito jajajaja' [well my boyfriend is half coastal and half highlander and how I looooove my *cholito* hahahaha]

xxxxnancy: 'Pobres mis paisanos peruanos que son indios con gente tan estupida y racista como esta negra o los mestizos que estan alli. Si estuvieran en USA estos racistas solo serian basura y lo que vale es la habilidad, educacion y talento y hay que luchar y estudiar mucho. Ojala desaparecieran los racistas de la faz de la tierra.' [My poor peruvian compatriots who are Indians, with such stupid and racist people like that black woman and the mestizos that are there. If they were in the USA those racists would just be garbage and what counts is ability, education and talent and you have to struggle and study a lot. I wish racists would disappear from the face of the earth]

Because of the open-ended structure of the YouTube dialogue, no one here has the last word, and the users appear to be aware of this as they continue to add further commentary, ignoring or responding to postings as they choose. The tone varies from authoritative, to playful, to offended, but in any case, there is always room for another response, another serious, humorous or ambiguous variation on prior commentary, or the opening of a new line of discussion. And as users can only be identified by what they write about themselves, since none of them have posted images, it is easy here to experience the malleability and ambiguity of racial, ethnic, gendered, and national characteristics, combined with a collective insistence on defining terms.

A number of scholars have signaled the generalized phenomenon of passing on the internet, noting that everyone who participates in cyberspace, even by logging on to a site 'as' him or herself, is in a sense passing. As Jennifer González describes, to note one example, 'much of the activity online is about becoming the fantasy of a racial other' (2000, p. 29). Hansen extends and transforms this argument, in order to suggest that the internet, new media, and in particular the work of artist Keith Piper, underscore a universalized corporeal affectivity that exceeds interpellation and fixed identity. In a radical move, Hansen argues that such media actually expose, 'the bankruptcy of the stereotyped media image and the categories of identity through which it previously performed its reifying cultural work' (2006, p. 141). His text thus points towards the promise that these media may hold, to reveal a collective and inclusive 'whatever body,' a concept he borrows from Agemben.

In the case of the YouTube videos and responses to Laura Bozzo's episodes that I discuss here, it may seem far-fetched to apply Hansen's reading of Agemben's 'whatever body.' This would imply seeing, in the circulation of images and definitions of the *cholo*, in the playful posturing of the 'Italian,' or in YouTube commentary, felicitous examples of, 'belonging to this impropriety as such … a singularity without identity, a common and absolutely exposed singularity … a communication without presuppositions and without subjects' (Hansen, 2006, p. 143). I would call the application of this reading here an exaggeration, not because of the radical difference in linguistic register and motivating interests between, for example, the Italian philosopher, and the 'Italian' suitor on Laura's program, but rather because in this particular episode and the online responses to it, ethnic and national specificity do retain some significance, even when categories are open to play and debate. Part of the importance of specificity here stems from the fact that both the program and the YouTube community are engaged in processes of transnational interpretation and translation. Luis Abanto Morales and Laura Bozzo both make reference to the Peruvian and Hispanic communities in the United States and elsewhere, who may be watching the program. In the case of YouTube, most of the users who comment on this sequence live in Europe or the United States. In many comments users specify that they come from a particular country or region, and therefore either have specific knowledge, or must ask for explanations from others who live elsewhere. In this sense – despite a degree of shared knowledge – ethnic, national and regional identities must be continuously redefined and interpreted, precisely because the pan-Hispanic imaginary which viewers and users purport to share is in fact intersected by multiple perspectives, realities that are both localized and heavily mediated through transnational cybernetic circuits. Thus if Hansen's notion of a 'whatever body' emerges here momentarily, it is nonetheless shot through repeatedly with the reiteration of specific subject identities; the network of user commentary serves both to open and shut down the boundaries of the body as subject: cholo, Italian, Peruvian, whatever, not necessarily in that order.

The partial opposition here between the specificity of national and ethnic identity, and the blurred, virtual, 'whatever' quality of these categories, appears to reiterate an important aspect of the structure and history of freak show spectacle, linked in turn to the history of the contemporary talk show, and to the notion of embarrassment I have discussed above. As mentioned, a central common element of the two genres is an insistence on truth and authenticity, grounded in material 'proof,' combined with the blurring of such proof through simulation, fraud, or ambiguity. The notion of 'mixed reality,' and the above-cited examples from YouTube, however, point to the possibility of reconsidering these oppositions.

The freak show and the television talk show form part of a historical trajectory of US mass entertainment, and both participate, as I have suggested here, in articulations and unpackings of embodied national and racial identities. In the case of Spanish-language talk shows in the Americas, however, the geopolitics of entertainment and information exchange have necessarily shifted. Such talk shows also evolved in part from the Anglo-American freak show, via the English language talk show (Monsiváis, 2000, p. 236). yet their construction and negotiation of oppositional or differential identities is far more complex, since their audience may include viewers from many different countries, as well as US Latinos. And in a sense, shows that are broadcast from Miami to a Latin American audience actually invert the dynamic of the traditional freak show or ethnographic spectacle, for rather than serving as a window for a mainstream US population on its geographically distant racial and cultural Others, such shows entertain Latin American communities by exposing them to the unfamiliar, and to some, bizarre and morally offensive behavior of Latinos in the United States (Monsiváis, 2000, p. 242). This shift is significant here, since the increased complexity and proliferation of identity categories prevents an absolute emptying of the 'husk' – to borrow from Hansen's use of the term – of ethnic-national identity. Instead, new content and new versions continually emerge to fill it, or in some cases to keep it in circulation as the empty object of enjoyment.

In conclusion, I look at an example from YouTube that does in fact come closer to an effective emptying of the stereotyped media image, thanks to its creative and unexpected engagement with the medium. In this case, rather than simply uploading segments of Laura's shows, the user has created a new video, incorporating brief clips from Laura. The entry opens with the following printed statement:

> Si tienes profesión, idiomas, eres educado, correcto, no cruzas una luz roja ni como peatón, y recojes la caquita de tu perro ... Toda esa buena impresión se puede terminar cuando alguien te pregunta ... Ya que eres peruano me puedes decir si ... ¿Es cierto todo lo que aparece en el programa de Laura Bozzo? [If you have a job, know some languages, you're educated and polite, you don't run red lights, even on foot, and you pick up after your dog ... all of this good impression can be destroyed when someone asks you ... 'since you're Peruvian, can you tell me if everything that appears on Laura Bozzo's show is real?']. (Feaso, 2006)

It is impossible to fully gauge the tone of the statement, since it appears silently, printed across the screen, distant from the shrill hype of the voices that call out their condemnation or approval of Laura, her show, and the images it ostensibly generates. It is no longer a matter of truth or falsehood, or even approval or condemnation, but in this case, the momentary erasure of a corporeal signifier, so that the viewer/reader's identification is severed from the violent, angry voices and bodies that circulate as inflated icons of Peruvian identity, in a pan-Hispanic media entertainment circuit. To borrow again from Hansen's reading, such a moment could be said to reveal the empty husk of a national image, exposing the absurdity of the classification of humans through 'social categories of visibility' (Hansen, 2006, p. 141).

The rest of the video is structured as a montage of segments from Laura's program, including the standard fare of marital infidelity and abuse, intercalated with footage from a different program ('La ventana indiscreta') showing Laura testifying on her alleged financial involvement with Vladimiro Montesinos. The soundtrack consists of a voiceover, describing Laura's activity, and dripping with sarcasm, as well as fragments from the programs and from Laura's testimony, and the 'Laura' theme song. At times, the sound is so heavily layered with the simultaneous recordings of all of these sources that it becomes difficult to separate one from the next, or to determine how the sound corresponds to the image on the screen. The images, in turn, are constructed through the filming of a television screen on which the shows are playing, and then a computer screen, so as to emphasize the external framing of the montage, or perhaps to dizzy the viewer in the blur from one format to the next. Although there is no question that the intention of this video is to attack and criticize Laura Bozzo for the negative image of Perú that her work has allegedly promoted, the organization of the piece also recirculates a series of increasingly familiar images through multiple frames, so that rather than a straightforward negation of stereotypes and condemnation of trash TV, the viewer experiences a hyper-saturated version of Laura. The rapid, jerking movements of her angry guests who beat upon one another, sometimes exposing bare flesh as clothing flies upwards, blends into the rhythm of the fast-paced montage, flipping from scene to scene, just as bodies blur into the frames that expose them, and the voiceover seems to echo – or to prompt – Laura's subtitled declaration from her television testimony: 'O sea que soy loca' [or in other words I'm crazy]. Or in other words, the body-voice image is momentarily freed from its status as condemnatory figure, and begins to operate both within and beyond its citational framework. The final text to appear on the screen of this video affirms that it is the mission of each of 'us' (Peruvians) to change the negative image of Perú in the world that Laura Bozzo has generated. The video itself already participates in this process, by exposing the talk show hostess as an exploitative charlatan. But in a more interesting sense, it accomplishes a shift in the relationship between national image and digital clip, by increasing the velocity of transition from body to context, and from one body to the next, so that frameworks blur – or bleed – into flesh. The audiences, participants, and YouTube users, in the meantime, are left to beat upon one another, or perhaps to fake it, and to grasp at anonymous limbs and shreds of clothing – whatever remains of an embarrassingly empty body.

As in the two juxtaposed Bozzo videos of the young, crying girl(s), described at the beginning of this essay, here too, the internet circulation of emotionally charged images – and repeated user interaction with these images – creates a partial emptying of image-content. What remains is not so much the visible spectacle of the bodies featured on the screen, as the calculated movement from one screen, or frame, to the next. And the split-second calculations become inseparable from the affective experience of the internet user. Rather than simply presenting an external, virtual body that might interpellate its viewers as Peruvians, indignant at Bozzo's offensive misrepresentation of their national and self images – although this still takes place to some degree – these clips suggest a realignment of supposed divisions between virtual and embodied subjects. The enjoyment, or embarrassment of internet viewing, intrinsic to the users' experience of these clips, is rooted, once again, in the body's technicity, in the exposure of a self-sustaining circuitry between viewer and framed image, so that the empty husk of stereotyped social visibility belongs as much to the flesh of the user as to the flickering screens.

Notes

1. Laura was placed under house arrest in 2002 for an alleged financial corruption scheme involving Vladimiro Montesinos, former aide to President Fujimori (Gotkine, 2003) and in 2006 was found guilty of embezzlement (Segura, 2006). The suggestion that Bozzo's show actually served Fujimori's political aims (Gotkine, 2003) further links her work to the former president's orchestrated populism, and to his violent regime.
2. As Ben Fritz and Michael Learmonth write, 'Many studios, labels and diskeries are busy taking full advantage of the ever growing promotional power of YouTube, particularly among the younger 18–24 demo, and are actually pushing the Netco to offer them more advertising options' (2007, para. 8). Also see 'Viacom will sue YouTube for $1bn' (2007), and 'About YouTube' (2007).
3. As Harvey Blume writes, in reference to freak show spectacles: 'The genres it was most crucial for Barnum to confound were those of fact and fiction, or, more specifically, science and showmanship' (1999, p. 191).

References

About YouTube. (2007). Retrieved 15 November 2007 from http://www.youtube.com/t/about

Blume, H. (1999). Ota Benga and the Barnum perplex. In B. Lindors (Ed.), *Africans on stage: Studies in ethnological show business* (pp. 188–202). Bloomington: Indiana UP.

Butler, J. (1993). *Bodies that matter*. New York: Routledge.

Callevip. (2007, May 27). Laura Bozo malogro la imagen del Peru. Retrieved 14 November 2007 from http://youtube.com/watch?v=eTEd99DTgKo

Daniperu25. (2007a, October 19). Cholo soy y no me compadezcas – Laura Bozzo (parte 1). Retrieved 14 November 2007 from http://youtube.com/watch?v=M0lTSe7rBqk

Daniperu25. (2007b, October 19). Laura Bozzo – Cholo soy y no me compadezcas (parte 2). Retrieved 14 November 2007 from http://youtube.com/watch?v=jPwgrb1oONQ

Daniperu25. (2007c, October 19). Laura Bozzo – Cholo soy y no me compadezcas (parte 3). Retrieved 14 November 2007 from http://youtube.com/watch?v=3q2Na5FGNxU

Daniperu25. (2007d, October 19). Laura Bozzo – Cholo soy y no me compadezcas (parte final). Retrieved 14 November 2007 from http://youtube.com/watch?v=OBbKil4hYZU

Eco, U. (1983). A guide to the neo-television of the 1980s. R. Lumley (Trans). In Z. Baranski & R. Lumley (Eds.), *Culture and conflict in postwar Italy* (pp. 245–255). New York: St Martin's Press.

Feaso. (2006, June 7). Laura Bozzo, la imagen del Perú en el mundo. Retrieved 14 November 2007 from http://youtube.com/watch?v =WaZoBqfIxco

Fritz, B, & Learmonth, M. (2007, March 10). Showbiz's site fright. Web seen as both a threat and a goldmine. Retrieved 15 November 2007 from *Variety*, http://www.variety.com/article/VR1117960880.html?categoryid =13&cs =1

Gamson, J. (1998). *Freaks talk back: Tabloid talk shows and sexual nonconformity.* Chicago: University of Chicago Press.

González, J. (2000). The appended subject: Race and identity as digital assemblage. In B. Kolko, L. Nakamura & G. Rodman (Eds.), *Race in cyberspace* (pp. 27–50). New York: Routledge.

Gotkine, E. (2003, May 8). Peru's 'Jerry Springer' battles scandal. Retrieved 15 November 2007 from http://news.bbc.co.uk/2/hi/americas/3012397.stm

Hansen, M. (2003). *New philosophy for new media.* Cambridge: MIT Press.

Hansen, M. (2006). *Bodies in code.* New York: Routledge.

Hayles, N.K. (2005). *My mother was a computer. Digital subjects and literary texts.* Chicago: University of Chicago Press.

Laudano, C. (1998). Talk shows: Entre la visualidad de la violencia y la invisibilización de la subordinación. [Talk shows: Between the visuality of violence and the invisibilization of subordination]. *Revista Feminaria, XI*(21), 34–42.

Monsiváis, C. (2000). *Aires de familia. Cultura y sociedad en América Latina.* [Family airs: Culture and society in Latin America]. Barcelona: Anagrama.

Ndigital. (2007, April 23). Jaime Bayly y Laura Bozzo (3/5). Retrieved 14 November 2007 from http://youtube.com/watch?v=Tnv_stPeQAk

Powerpollito. (2007, August 23). Sismo Perú: ¿Laura Bozzo en Pisco? (Magaly TeVe 21-08-2007). Retrieved 14 November 2007, from http://youtube.com/watch?v=9OHmppn_YUU

Provincia. (2007, February 28). Laura Bozzo La gran ayudadora. Retrieved 14 November 2007, from http://youtube.com/watch?v=eywEyNF7zRc

Segura, A. (2006). Laura Bozzo condenada a prisión. Retrieved 15 November 2007 from http://latino.msn.com/entretenimiento/television/articles/articlepage.aspx?cp-documentid=645203

Sheenny (2007, November 8). Denuncia Laura Bozzo – ¿falsa panelista? (Prensa Libre). Retrieved 16 September 2008 from http://www.youtube.com/watch?v=Y3eC9kV91fs

Siebers, T. (2004). Words stare like a glass eye: From literary to visual to disability studies and back again. *PMLA, 119*(5), 1315–1324.

Sobchack, V. (2004). *Carnal thoughts: Embodiment and moving image culture.* Berkeley: University of California Press.

Tolson, A. (2001). Talking about talk: The academic debates. In A. Tolson (Ed.), *Television talk shows: Discourse, performance, spectacle* (pp. 1–30). Mahwah, NJ: Lawrence Erlbaum Publishers.

Viacom Will Sue YouTube for $1bm. (2007, March 13). Retrieved 15 November 2007 from BBC News, http://news.bbc.co.uk/2/hi/business/6446193.stm

Žižek, S. (2005). *Violencia en acto. Conferencias en Buenos Aires.* [Violence in act: Conferences in Buenos Aires]. A. Hounie (Comp.), P. Willson (Trans.). Buenos Aires: Paidós.

Digital ghosts, global capitalism and social change

Freya Schiwy

Media and Cultural Studies Department, University of California, Riverside, USA

This article traces the importance of colonial legacies for theorizing speculative capitalism by thinking from the use of digital media by indigenous social movements in the Andes. Indeed, rather than marginal to global capitalism, I maintain that indigenous peoples and media activists are at the forefront of experimenting with political and economic alternatives to capitalism. I argue that the racialized body remains tangible as digital media are read and used akin to older, analogue technology and its 'writing of light.' The desires for truth and corporeality in indigenous media point to the existence of borders from which alternatives to the current capitalist order are imagined and enacted. Similarly, in indigenous films speculative capitalism betrays its colonial constitution that ties it back to modern/colonial economic forms, rather than creating an entirely novel break with the past. In light of indigenous media digital images and the notion of immaterial labor are haunted by similar, colonial ghosts.

A growing number of voices contend that we have entered a new global phase of history, that we are experiencing a technological revolution akin to that of the industrial revolution and the age of mechanical reproduction. Michael Hardt and Antonio Negri are not the only ones who see this transformation of emphasis from industrial production to the stock market as a sign of a new phase and form of capitalism and a paradigm shift with regard to modernity. One of its consequences, they argue, is that both imperialism and colonialism have reached their end and actually become counterproductive (Hardt & Negri, 2000, p. 200). Instead of an exploitation and repression of ethnic differences, global capital celebrates and incorporates difference (p. 201). More recently, and despite his misgivings of Hardt and Negri, Mark Poster concurs that the digital domain along with transnational corporate capitalism inaugurates a new globalization. Even granting certain continuities – such as the ongoing global dominance of Europe and the USA – he suggests that 'the current situation of globalization, spearheaded by transnational corporations, might best be comprehended not from a standpoint of postcolonialism but from one that takes its point of departure from emergent forms of domination' (Poster, 2006, p. 27). This article examines the intersections of digital media, immaterial labor, and desires for the tangible that linger across the alleged paradigm shift. In contrast with Poster I argue that, upon closer examination, digital images and the notion of immaterial labor are haunted by similar, colonial ghosts.

Understanding the characteristics of the information age and what it means to act politically in these conditions has acquired a sharply-felt urgency. Indigenous movements in Bolivia, for example, have been protesting against neoliberal reforms, such as the attempted privatization of water and natural gas. They are debating strategies for eliminating the rampant poverty of large parts of the population. Living standards have declined with neoliberalism and many are realizing that capitalism cannot fulfill its promises. These same movements elected Evo Morales, Latin America's first indigenous president, who took office in January 2006. One of his first acts of state was to call a Constituent Assembly in August 2006. The Assembly allowed for contentious negotiations between traditional elites and social movement representatives who desire new models of state and economy. Alternative proposals are inspired by the work of organizations such as the Aymara Movement to Reconstitute the *Ayllu*, that has revived Quechua and Aymara forms of governance and market relations in the highlands (Choque Quispe & Mamani Condori, 2003, pp. 147–67; Stephenson, 2002) as well as by indigenous movement organizations like CIDOB (Confederación de los Pueblos Indígenas de Bolivia), which represents a majority of the eastern lowlands indigenous peoples in Bolivia (see http://www.cidob-bo.org/).[1]

Indigenous media activists of diverse ethnic origins have played an important role in communicating the culturally diverse peoples of the region. For over a decade and following a carefully planned strategy, they have used digital video technology in order to strengthen cultural traditions. CAIB (Coordinadora Audiovisual Indígena de Bolivia) and CEFREC (Centro de Formación y Realización Cinematográfica) conceived the National Indigenous Plan for Audiovisual Communication in 1996 (see http://videoindigena.bolnet.bo). The plan, which has remained independent of the Bolivian State, is supported by all the major indigenous organizations and peasant unions in Bolivia, that is, by those who have issued alternative proposals during the Constituent Assembly (*Asamblea, 2006*).[2] As part of the plan, the activists created a video and community television network that regularly distributed digital video and multimedia packages to a growing number of villages in the Bolivian highlands and the transnational Amazon basin. Making use of subtitles and simultaneous interpreting during scheduled screenings in the villages, indigenous media activists connect distant rural villages across cultural and language differences (see Schiwy, 2009, chapter 1). Multimedia packages containing indigenous-made radio and television shows as well as documentary and fiction shorts have been instrumental in preparing these communities to actively participate in the public debate about a new constitution in Bolivia. The multimedia package 'Rumbo a la Asamblea Constituyente', for instance, directly informs about indigenous rights and strategies that can impact on the Constituent Assembly. Facilitated by digital media, the communication process among culturally very distinct indigenous communities has led villagers to diagnose and critique the dominance of discourses that continue to locate them as impediments to development and to Bolivia's entry into full-scale modernity.

With unprecedented self-confidence, a wide range of indigenous organizations are claiming the relevance of forms of knowledge, economy, and governance that have been subalternized in a long colonial history, which from this vantage point has not yet ended. 'Domination,' writes the Bolivian political theorist Pablo Mamani Ramírez, 'is colonial because indigenous peoples are conceptualized as subjects without history and without technological resources. It is modern because capital, which produces modern industrial technology, exploits indigenous subjects as a social class' (Mamani Ramírez, 2006, p. 37). In other words, from the perspective of indigenous movements emerges a profound doubt whether we can begin to understand what is happening by casting colonial legacies to the side. Reshaping the global economy apparently demands decolonization.[3]

Why privilege such a site for analyzing the intersection of digital media and global capitalism? Oftentimes indigenous peoples are seen as marginal, perhaps even as inhabiting a delayed entry point into the digital age. Some suggest that the experience of virtual reality, digital communication, and the abstract volatility of stock markets that create a sense of living in a disembodied world have little impact on the majority of the world's populations who don't even have access to the telephone (Hayles, 1999, p. 20). While we certainly do not all play virtual reality games to the same extent, the pervasion of cell phone technology, television, film, even access to the internet have been growing exponentially (Poster, 2006, pp. 38–45; Miller, Govil, McMurria, Maxwell, & Wang, 2005; Sinclair & Turner 2004). Even as participation in the global financial markets remains limited, global economic policies and crises are surely affecting even the most rural places. Geopolitically anchored temporal divisions that divide global regions into premodern, modern, and postmodern realms, on the other hand, betray a legacy of colonial thinking. The association of indigenous peoples with backwardness indicates a blind spot at the heart of our efforts to understand global capitalism. Digital media are allowing for the creation of expanding communication networks among often times remote rural areas. Rather than in the backwaters of Wall Street and the emerging global cities, indigenous peoples in Latin America are at the forefront of experimenting with political and economic alternatives to global capitalism.

Digital disembodiment and ontological longing

The avowed paradigm shift in global capitalism is linked to the sense of a growing abstraction and disembodiment spanning communication, representation, and the creation of value. Digital video technology, for instance, appears to have radically changed the way sound and images are recorded. No longer, as with analogue recording, does it veritably carve onto tape the hills and valleys of light (Rodowick, 2001, p. 1399). No longer does reality leave a tactile trace of the ephemeral, 'a molding, the taking of an impression, by the manipulation of light' as André Bazin (1974, p. 12) put it when he likened analogue photography to the making of a death mask. Digital technology appears disembodied and instantaneous, in so far as it is comprised of algorithmic functions that can easily be reproduced, transmitted, and altered. As Rodowick explains: 'Digital production renders all expressions identical since they are all reducible to the same computational basis. The basis of all such "representation" is virtuality, mathematical abstractions that render all signs equivalent regardless of their output medium' (Rodowick, 2001, p. 1399). Poster concurs: 'Texts, images, and sounds now travel at the speed of electrons and may be altered at any point along their course. They are as fluid as water and simultaneously present everywhere' (Poster, 2006, p. 24).

This celebration of virtuality is linked to the cybernetic understanding of electronic communication and artificial intelligence. Cybernetics suggests that human beings be comprehended as information processing entities, ontologically akin to intelligent machines. Participants in the Macy Conferences on Cybernetics (held from 1943 to 1954) cast humans as autonomous entities and then quickly began to conceive of them as entities characterized by feedback loops. Now they are seen as autopoeitic systems created by mutually constitutive interactions. Although cybernetics thus accounts for complex forms of relations it has increasingly sedimented the idea that mind and body are separate and that human consciousness resides in the mind alone (see Hayles, 1999, pp. 7–11). Following Kathryn Hayles' insights, the discourse of cybernetics, however, displays a fundamental ambiguity. By insisting on the separation of mind and body it in fact reiterates a dominant and very modern paradigm that has been challenged by feminist, postcolonial, and – I would add – anti-colonial theories put forth by indigenous intellectuals. As Hayles puts it,

> the erasure of embodiment is a feature common to both the liberal humanist subject and the cybernetic posthuman... Although in many ways the posthuman deconstructs the liberal humanist subject, it thus shares with its predecessor an emphasis on cognition rather than embodiment... To the extent that the posthuman constructs embodiment as the instantiation of thought/information, it continues the liberal tradition rather than disrupts it. (1999, pp. 4–5)

Digital video's work of abstraction can be similarly challenged. The medium remains anchored in labor processes that manifest themselves in the products and materials employed in recording and distribution as well as in the actual work of video and film making (see Hayles, 2005). The working body is a ghostly presence here. Equally important, digital video's algorithmic codes are jarringly in dissonance with the lingering and stubborn, modern longing for truth in audiovisual images. We still believe ourselves to be seeing a true image of a person or object framed, even in fiction films. In documentary films and television news reports this effect is magnified. Like in testimonial literature, truthfulness in terms of an ontological rendering of reality is part of the documentary expectation, no matter how aware we are of the fact that audiovisual images, regardless of recording technology, have always been constructed through camera angle and distance, lighting, the editing process, and so forth.

Digital video continues to work its documentary effect across diverse cultures of viewing. Consider a set of examples from indigenous media.[4] CEFREC-CAIB's documentaries and news shows rarely strive to destabilize the truth claims of documentary film. Instead, for many indigenous communicators in Bolivia, digital technology serves a crucial indexical purpose: to document rituals, agricultural practices, historical testimonials, and to denounce abuses and lies, such as in the environmental pollution caused by corporate oil companies. The Bolivian indigenous media activists prefer expository and interactive documentaries with alternating talking heads, even explicitly didactic and educational formats, because they permit straightforward address.[5] At the same time, however, the video makers are acutely aware that it matters who makes a film. In other words, far from a naive approach to film as a window upon reality, video makers wield the camera to reflect a different angle upon reality.

A short video self-representation of the National Indigenous Plan for Audiovisual Communication – *Pueblos Indigenas, Así Pensamos/Indigenous Peoples, This is how we Think* – for example, does not opt for self-reflection or a long, complex rendering of the history and context of indigenous media production. Instead *Pueblos Indígenas* focuses on several CAIB members who are framed separately, set against diverse landscapes, and who perform their ethnic identity through clothing and language use. Each video maker comments briefly on the problems concerning his or her community and how the process of audiovisual communication helps the community in dealing with remarkably similar issues. The footage is edited into a series of alternating 'talking bodies' where the media activists speak not only for themselves but for the diversity of indigenous peoples involved in the plan. The video relies on the spectators taking the performance of those on screen at face value. These spectators are in the majority rural indigenous viewers who are watching their peers, rather than development experts sent by the State or non-governmental organizations. Although filmed in digital format, the preference for conventional documentary form builds on an implied contract between viewers and film makers. The contract is bolstered by what Charles Peirce called the 'indexical bond' between screen representation and referent: 'The bond between representation and referent, that is, between the image and the real world, produces an impression of authenticity which documentary draws on as a warrant or guarantee of the accuracy and authority of its representation' (Beattie, 2004, p. 13). In other words, this contract stipulates that what we see is indeed what is there and that what the commentators say is factual.

Indigenous documentaries thus counter a dominant colonial gaze. In ethnographic film white colonizers and scientists have objectified colonial others and bound viewers into their desires and anxieties. As E. Ann Kaplan writes,

> the gaze of the colonialist thus refuses to acknowledge its own power and privilege: it unconsciously represses knowledge of power hierarchies and its need to dominate, to control. Like the male gaze, it's an objectifying gaze, one that refuses mutual gazing, mutual subject-to-subject recognition. It refuses what I am calling a 'looking relation'. (Kaplan, 1997, p. 79)[6]

Indigenous documentaries, in contrast, bind subjects, film makers, and spectators into the same realm of reality. The documentary shorts *K'anchariy. Para Encender la Luz del Espíritu/Kanchariy. Lighting up the Spirit* and *Rebeldías y Esperanzas/ Rebellions and Hopes* further highlight the video makers' conviction that research dynamics and ends are changed when the video maker is indigenous. In *K'anchariy* the Aymara actor and director Reynaldo Yujra travels to the Quechua speaking Kallawaya in Northern Bolivia in order to learn about their medical practices. The video stages an alternative filmmaker figure, distinct from the anthropologist and situated on the same side of the 'colonial difference' (Mignolo, 2000, p. 13; 2002, p. 221) as the community that he visits. The information obtained, at the same time, becomes part of an indigenous intercultural exchange instead of being integrated into the anthropological archive. *Rebeldías*, directed by the Quechua Marcelina Cárdenas from the southern Bolivian region of Potosí, compares weaving practices. Here a fictional character from the highlands travels to a village in the lowlands investigating and comparing women's weavings. Her visit leads to an exchange which the woman from the lowlands reciprocates with a visit to Potosí. In both the documentary *K'anchariy* and the docudrama *Rebeldías*, the scenes of encounter between indigenous media activists and members of the community are re-enacted. Yet both *K'anchariy* and *Rebeldías* at once appeal to the ontological dimension of mutual recognition captured on screen. The film's indexicality is the basis for intra-racial looking relations on screen and beyond.

Intercultural communication thus constructs sameness where indigenous peoples see each other and themselves on screen. As I have argued elsewhere, they affirm the survival of indigenous cultures and address problems that often transcend the particular situation of individual communities (Schiwy, 2009). This response to the colonial encoding of vision relies on the factual contract of documentary realism, regardless of the change in technology from analogue to digital. While digital recording's mathematical codes uncouple the image from what is in front of the lens, in viewing digital images audiences continue to insist on an indexicality that 'proves' indigenous communities to already inhabit the digital age.

Immaterial labor and life itself

Similar and indeed related to the arguments about the virtual nature of digital technology, others contend that the products of labor and our interaction with machines has also fundamentally changed. Mauricio Lazzarato (1996) argued that the industrial production process relies more and more on immaterial labor – thought, planning, creativity – instead of on physical labor and machines. Antonio Negri affirms the key impact that results from the reform of the financial system under Nixon and Kissinger in 1971 and from the change in forms of production (Negri, 2003, pp. 32–33). Transnational corporate capitalism now generates much of its profit through speculation (stocks, land, information) made possible by new digital communication technologies. Frederic Jameson maintains that abstraction (money) has been taken to a higher level: 'Globalization is rather a kind of cyberspace in which money capital has reached its ultimate dematerialization as messages which pass instantaneously from one nodal point to another across the former globe, the former material world' (Jameson, 2000, p. 154).[7] Robert Reich (2007, p. 96) includes a graph representing the increase in share values and trading volume at the global financial trading centers, a staggering visualization of the changes that are occurring in the financial sector as well as its exponentially increasing importance. Along with these changes many see a rearticulation of what it means to act politically.

Hardt and Negri (2000, p. 32) suggest that the deployment and consumption of information, cultural performances and intellectual debates are inherent to the capitalist system, constituting a plane of immanence. Immaterial labor indicates that capitalism has assimilated not only labor power but emotions and intellectual production.[8] Critique and transformation hence no longer come from the outside. The alternatives to the global system arise precisely from within. In a manner resembling Foucault's totalizing and sometimes misunderstood notion of power, the rhizomatic distribution of power and sites of immaterial labor constitute both moments of self-policing or 'control' as well as occasions for transforming the system. If Foucault's concept of power entailed resistance, immaterial labor's immanence to the system allows only for an *inherent* transformation: 'the creative forces of the multitude that sustain Empire are also capable of autonomously constructing a counter-Empire, an alternative political organization of global flows and exchanges' (Hardt & Negri, 2000, p. xv).

27

The concept of immaterial labor, for Hardt and Negri achieves thus a double move. On the one hand, it extends the Marxist concept of the proletariat to a global level that is no longer anchored in industrial labor; on the other hand it extends the Foucaultian idea of biopolitics to an all-encompassing experience. As if trying to ground the virtuality of immaterial labor, Hardt and Negri reclaim the ontological dimension of life. They state that

> in the biopolitical context of Empire ... the production of capital converges ever more with the production and reproduction of social life itself; it thus becomes ever more difficult to maintain distinctions among productive, reproductive, and unproductive labor. Labor – material or immaterial, intellectual or corporeal – produces and reproduces social life, and in the process is exploited by capital. (p. 402)

Since social forces, or rather social life in its entirety, produce the responses of global capitalism, the ontological dimension of life grounds the possibilities for positive change, not only the exercise of power from above but also a productive biopower that transforms the world from below.

The sense that something lingers informs not only digital media production and reception but also Hardt and Negri's analysis of global capitalism and biopower. On the one hand, there is a wish to understand and perceive what is novel, whether in digital technology or in what Hardt and Negri call virtual capitalism. Privileging what is new is of course itself a modern sensibility. What lingers is also a modern desire for grounding life in the ontology of being. (The modern discourse of knowledge abstracting from the body notwithstanding.) I would suggest this lingering betrays a doubt: the paradigm shift apparently indicated by global capitalism and digital technology may not be as radical as it seems.

The problem lies instead in how this ontology of being is conceived. If we think of being in abstraction, uncoupled from the way subjectivity has been constituted through discourses and practices, all forms of creating links and social life become potentially transformative (see Colectivo Situaciones, 2002, p. 26). Grounding the constitution of global capitalism historically and in connection with the production of subjectivity, however, creates a different outlook. The consciousness of a global world and the establishment of global trade and exploitation in the sixteenth century rely on what we might also call immaterial labor – the colonial discourses on humanity and later race (indeed the cross fertilization of gender and racial stereotypes) that served to justify geopolitical structures of economic exploitation. In short, the problem with globalization is not merely one of capital accumulation. Hardt and Negri would not disagree on that. As Santiago Castro-Gómez has pointed out, for Hardt and Negri

> it is precisely in the enlightened project of normalization where colonialism fits so well. Constructing the profile of the 'normal' subject that capitalism needed (white, male, owner, worker, heterosexual, etc.) necessarily required the image of an 'other' located in the exteriority of European space. The identity of the bourgeois subject in the 17th century is constructed in opposition to the image of 'savages' who lived in America, Africa, and Asia that chroniclers and travelers had circulated throughout Europe. (Castro-Gómez, 2007, pp. 429–30)

For Hardt and Negri, however, colonialism and postcolonialism remain derivative of modernity and postmodernity, not constitutive of them (Mignolo, 2002, p. 228). Yet colonialism and the control of the Atlantic are not byproducts of an industrial capitalism developed in European nation states. Rather they give rise to a global world system and a structure of power – the 'coloniality of power' – that is constitutive of global capitalism as such (Mignolo, 2002, pp. 227–34; Castro-Gómez, 2007, p. 435). As Quijano and Wallerstein put it, 'the Americas were not incorporated into an already existing capitalist world economy. There could not have been a capitalist world-economy without the Americas' (1992, p. 549).

The modern/colonial life of digital images

Like Hardt and Negri, Poster's work on new technologies sets off the heritage of colonialism from 'the larger phenomenon of globalization.' He asks,

> from the standpoint of the former colonies of Europe, the United Sates, and Japan, also known as the postcolonial nations, can it be said that the chief hegemonic power limiting their freedom is the heritage of colonialism, or is it rather the spreading and deepening tentacles of globalization? (Poster, 2006, p. 26)

In other words, even if colonialism may have been foundational to the global capitalist world system, Poster argues that colonialism no longer explains forms oppression and exploitation currently on the rise:

> Many, if not most, of the colonized nations of the Western imperial epoch from 1500–1950 continue to suffer from subordinate relations with the United States and Europe. Even granting these continuities with the past, the current situation of globalization, spearheaded by transnational corporations, might best be comprehended not from a standpoint of postcolonialism but from one that takes its point of departure from emergent forms of domination. (p. 27)

When Poster argues that colonialism no longer informs emergent forms of domination he invokes a simplified postcolonial theory that opposes colonizer and colonized and that contrasts with a globalization spearheaded by 'the processes of economics, migration and communication' (p. 28). Yet these are by no means new phenomena. The global economy has been built on colonial exploitation, most migration itself is evidence of the continued global economic inequalities inaugurated with the global capitalist system that the conquest of the Americas initiates. Communication has from the start been part of an immaterial labor practice that justified colonial expansion and economic dominance and today trails modern/colonial legacies imbedded in its core.

The coloniality of power is an overarching paradigm that transcends the particular experience of modern colonialism (military occupation and economic exploitation with the key support of nation states). Constituted in the sixteenth century, coloniality references a complex structure of power that connects capital (economic exploitation structured geopolitically), subjectivity (the construction of race and gender imaginaries that seek to justify geopolitical and ethnic hierarchies) and epistemology (the uneven flows of knowledge and the global hegemony of a European genealogy of science, philosophy, and academic disciplines) (see Quijano & Wallerstein, 1992; Mignolo, 2000; Escobar, 2007; Schiwy, 2007).

Immaterial labor is crucial to capitalism whether as a direct source of value or as an indirect constitutive force of its imaginary. Immaterial labor and biopower, whether we conceive of it ontologically or in a poststructuralist sense as the metaphoric and material effects of discourse, are, in this sense, not novel elements of global capitalism, even if their importance for the creation of value has increased exponentially. Indeed, as Castro-Gómez argues, current bio-prospecting and international patent rights, together with an apparent interest in preserving biodiversity and the traditional knowledges of indigenous peoples re-enacts forms of exploitation and epistemic hierarchies that were already established. According to Castro-Gómez,

> 95 percent of the biological patents are controlled by five big biotechnical companies, and the earnings produced by the issuing of patents was fifteen thousand million dollars [sic] [15 billion US dollars] in 1990. The patents are the juridical mechanism by which new forms of colonial expropriation of knowledge are legitimated. (2007, p. 442)

Donna Haraway (1997) made a similar argument in *Modest Witness*. In chapter four of this book she showed how colonial racial-gender tropes are recycled in the advertisements of bioprospecting companies. Even Poster argues that digital technology is not all dematerialized but effects a qualitative fusion of human and machine that gives way to a 'humachine,' a joining of subject and object that forms the media's unconsciousness (Poster, 2006, p. 36). In the case of digital film and video this unconsciousness points to the body's persistent presence, a presence that, in my view, indicates colonial-looking relations at the heart of apparently disembodied forms of communication and the global exploitation of information.

Visual and later audiovisual images have long been a key element of the coloniality of power. Digital images transmitted daily on television and the internet resonate not only with a desire for indexicality, but also with an audiovisual archive that has been shaped by analogue film and its complicity with capitalist and colonialist imaginaries. While Stanley Aronowitz (1979) had termed analogue film the art form of capitalism, Ella Shohat and Robert Stam argue that cinema supplied the tool for visualizing the tropes and metaphors of conquest put forth by popular exhibitions and works of fiction, thus continuing the spread of enthusiasm for the imperial projects beyond the elites and into the popular strata (Shohat & Stam, 1994, p. 100). Film has been instrumental in performing itself as a technology indicative of modernity and development in a western mode. On screen and off it has subalternized alternative forms of life and understanding. Film has co-produced affects and a geopolitical reality shaped by economic exploitation. The construction of race, epistemic privilege, and temporal differences manifesting themselves across space have constituted the product of film's immaterial labor. In fiction films this emplotment is particularly powerful because of the way emotion and desire compel the viewer. Far from receding from the current global capitalist imaginary and despite innovative experiments in ethnographic filmmaking, audiences are still captivated by recent box office hits such as *King Kong* and *Apocalypto* that prolong the discourse of globalization inherited from the sixteenth century as they re-enact colonial fantasies through computer generated images – that is, mathematical codes – which enable compelling special effects. Indigenous and western audiences certainly experience film in an ambiguous manner, at once in its ontological quality and in its artifice. Often enough the desire for ontology continues to resonate with the well-rehearsed theme of colonial subordination. While finance capitalism currently obtains its greatest, albeit fictional, gains from virtual money transfers, stock purchases and so forth, concentrating on this aspect alone risks obscuring the way the coloniality or 'postcoloniality' of power continues to drive global capitalism.

Keeping this legacy in mind, in contrast, helps to discern more specifically when and how the global system is currently being challenged and reshaped.

Border economy

What remains in question then, are the implications for political action at a time when global capitalism is indeed propelled by immaterial labor. If we can now assert that the 'new' global capitalism is still shaped by colonial legacies, what happens to the forms and places of critical transformation? Does the plane of immanence cover 'the entire world market and global society' (Negri, 2003, p. 45)? Is transformation achieved by the social relations that would form an exodus from the State and from Work, as Paulo Virno has it (2005, p. 5)?

The critical discourse articulated through indigenous media in Bolivia proposes again a slightly different view. In the award-winning fiction short *Qati Qati/Whispers of Death* the actors perform an Aymara economy based on barter, a self-sufficiency and independence from industrial products that is in great part tied to the woman's body. As if visualizing the Quechua/Aymara moral imperative – *ama sua, ama lulla, ama kella* (do not steal, do not lie, do not be lazy) – physical labor is an overwhelming presence in this film.[9] This representation of labor is coupled with references to a particular system of exchange. In a short scene, Valentina (Ofelia Condori) lends a neighbor *aji* and salt, even though the neighbor denies having visited Valentina in the form of a *qati qati*, or 'flying head', the night before. The figure of the *qati qati*, a digital ghost if you like, refers to a spirit that reciprocity appeases. In a broader sense, the scene encapsulates the ethics of a socio-economic system that finds its extension in wider ethnic relations implied in another scene: When Valentina goes to the market, she trades her highland potatoes for apricots, grown at warmer, lower elevations. The video *Qati Qati* thus conjures a 'vertical economy' of extended kinship networks that trade agricultural produce through the diverse ecological zones of the Andes (Murra, 2002, pp. 83–142). The market scene in *Qati Qati* directly invokes what Brooke Larson calls the 'adaptive vitality' (Larson, 1995, p. 12) of indigenous communities, where a monetary economy coexists with kinship-based relations of barter and exchange. The actors thus perform on screen the ideals of Andean society/economy: 'ecological complementarity, self-sufficiency, and reciprocity' (p. 13), or what Silvia Rivera Cusicanqui terms a 'reciprocal economy' (1996, p. 168).

Qulqi Chaliku/Silver Vest, also filmed in the Aymara speaking highlands, brings monetary exchange to the forefront, criticizing its excesses. *Qulqi* shows a market place where cattle and other livestock are traded for money. The film's protagonist, Satuco (Reynaldo Yujra), secretly sews wads of colorful Bolivian pesos into the liner of his vest, threadbare from age. In this fiction short, death punishes the protagonist for his avarice, after he confides his secret wealth to Cihualcollo (Jesús Tapia). Cihualcollo in turn robs Satuco's grave and, seeking political power in the community, invests the money in livestock. Yet haunted by Satuco's ghost, Cihualcollo loses his mind. *Qulqi*'s protagonists are punished harshly for their avarice and self-interested accumulation with death and insanity. The film criticizes the desire (prevalent among many in the communities) to become part of a capitalist society that seeks individual wealth and profit maximization.

Well aware that video making and distribution are forms of both immaterial and material labor and subject to market exchange, the media activists prolong the enactment of socio-economic ethics on screen in the making and distribution of indigenous media. Members of the indigenous organization of audiovisual communicators (CAIB) insist that the production of indigenous video is a communal effort. Marcelino Pinto from the coca growing Chapare region of Bolivia, for instance, is responsible for the script and directing of *El Oro Maldito/Cursed Gold* and for improvising a traveling shot during the video's climatic escape scene. Before *El Oro* was accepted for production, his colleagues in the CEFREC-CAIB crew rejected Pinto's earlier scripts several times, arguing that they were not promoting a positive self-image or were too risky in the national and international climate of the war on drugs. Pinto asserts therefore that the film is the result of a collaboration between CEFREC, CAIB, and the community that participated in the filming:

> The first script I wrote was based o the legend of the coca leaf, written by a Bolivian author. But that script didn't work because it implied that the coca leaf was evil, that it caused misfortune and led to death. So I threw that script aside. Then I did another, which was more like a denunciation, where the soldiers and the campesinos act out conflicts as they often happen there. But CAIB and CEFREC saw that it was premature to make that sort of video in what was and is a very tense time. Since the majority decides, they opted to make *El Oro Maldito*, a traditional fairy tale that functions on the metaphorical level. It was selected by all of the indigenous peoples. (Flores, 2001–02, p. 35)

The process of collectively deciding on scripts, editing, and postproduction submits itself to the structure of authority in the communities, to the communities' needs, and the cultural politics of indigenous social movements (see Schiwy, 2009).

Reynaldo Yujra similarly emphasized collective production during the international indigenous film festival in New York in 2000. Yet he stressed that the idea for the script of *Qati Qati* is based in oral tradition, that is, in legendary stories that do not assume an individual author but a long history of oral narrators. But Yujra also inscribes his responsibility for the film on screen. During the establishing shots in *Qati Qati*, viewers briefly glimpse a close-up profile of Yujra's face, illuminated by the blue moonlight that introduces the mysterious ambient of this horror tale. Yujra's enactment of the director figure in *K'anchariy* and *Qati Qati* points to the coexistence individualism and collective subjectivity that are linked through processes of reciprocity and responsibility.

While the audiovisual communicators of CAIB eschew the term 'director,' they nevertheless see a need to take individual responsibility for the final version of the video. Thus, Marcelina Cárdenas is responsible for *Llanthupi Munakuy*, Faustino Peña for *El Espíritu de la Selva*, Patricio Luna for *Qulqi Chaliku*, etc. CEFREC-CAIB prefers using the term 'responsable' to that of 'director' in order to mark the difference from the western director-star as well as from the Third Cinema director-collective that maintained focus on the revolutionary vanguard and its leadership, in this case, the names of filmmakers that have become icons in their own right (e.g. Jorge Sanjinés, Glauber Rocha, Octavio Getino, Fernando Solanas, Fernado Birri, Tomás Gutiérrez Alea, etc.). Indigenous media activists largely reject the romantic and marketable notion of the auteur and artist-creator who expresses his or her personality through the medium in favor of a conceptualization that is more adequate to the 'proceso integral' that constitutes indigenous video making

(Himpele, 2004, p. 358).[10] Yet at the same time, the video makers embrace the collective label 'indigenous video,' emphasizing their access to the technology and responsibility for the films.

Video production extends traditions of shared labor, *mit'a* or *minga*, where the community works together in harvests or hunting, but also in the construction of schoolhouses, churches, or roads.[11] The product of this labor entails complicated notions of property rights and maintains markers of reciprocity and barter that correspond to local socio-economic understandings. In an interview with the Salvadorian filmmaker Daniel Flores y Ascencio, member of CAIB Julia Mosúa (from San Francisco de Moxos in the lowlands of the Beni) insisted that her community, who participated in the acting and oral history gathered for her docufiction *Nuestra Palabra: Historia de San Francisco de Moxos/Our Word: The History of San Francisco de Moxos*, considered these images a product of their gratuitous labor (Flores, 2001–02, p. 31). Mosúa expressed that some in the community view her travels to film festivals with great suspicion (p. 32). Some community members (but not all) insistently argue against her or CEFREC's right to sell the videos, raising the issue of financial reimbursement for their participation in the filming, or simply denying CEFREC the right to circulate the images beyond circuits approved by the community representatives (Mosúa, Copa, & Pinto, 2000, n.p.).

In contrast, Alfredo Copa, Quechua from the highland region of Potosí, explained that his community considered their images, obtained for the documentary *Desemplovando Nuestra Historia/Dusting off our History*, the property of CEFEC-CAIB, that is of the producers and the multicultural organization of indigenous media activists. *Desempolvando* responded to the community's desire to rescue their elder's knowledge transmitted in storytelling, but the community also participated in the production as part of *ayni* (reciprocity) (Mosúa, Copa, & Pinto, 2000, n.p.). Alfredo Copa thus affirmed his ties with his rural community of origin. He is required, in turn, to reciprocate with manual labor (to participate in the construction of houses, for instance) as well as in his intellectual capacity. He may be called upon to mediate administrative issues with the state, to help voice his community's demands to the outside, and to continue to make video available (Mosúa, Copa, & Pinto, 2000; Flores, 2001–02, pp. 33–34). Participation in CAIB, which the communities support, must therefore be carefully balanced with other responsibilities, an issue, moreover, that limits the participation of women with child-care responsibilities.

Distribution, on the other hand, follows mixed market strategies. Videos are distributed regularly free of charge among the communities. The villagers reciprocate by providing places to sleep and food for the indigenous facilitators who carry the multi-media packages and, when necessary, equipment and generators. At indigenous film and video festivals no admission is charged. CEFREC-CAIB's videos have never been available in the free market because of concerns over intellectual property rights, as Mosúa laid out. When videos were still sold selectively, buyers were often screened as to their intended use of the material. The purchase frequently does not end with the exchange of money for a product. The distribution constitutes relationships that may include further obligations and responsibilities. CEFREC-CAIB covers the costs of cameras and other hardware as well as some staff positions in the production centers with grants obtained from non-governmental organizations (such as Mugarik Gabe from the Bask Country) or even from state institutions (such as AECI of the Spanish State). Indigenous media suggest that capitalism has incompletely permeated the Andean economy and that alternatives need to be thought from the ties between reciprocal economy and a community ethos anchored in stories about ghosts, flying heads, and enchanted waterfalls that many in the communities themselves have begun to consider superstitions.

Whether capitalism has entailed the wholesale integration and thus destruction of indigenous social and economic life or whether, on the contrary, marginalized indigenous communities have been able to maintain much of their aboriginal forms of production and exchange has also been a subject of scholarly debate. Although there was a profound shift toward the creation of more expansive regional and export economies in the twentieth century that demanded different modalities of negotiating their integration from peasant communities, anthropologists still find evidence 'against broad teleological notions of progressive market penetration and dislocation in the southern highlands . . . Andean commerce complemented but never displaced, traditional trading alliances that moved crops, salt, and livestock between valley and puna' (Larson, 1995, p. 33). Pre-colonial socio-economic relations – particularly those built around the ethical ideal of reciprocity, or *ayni* as it is called in Aymara, became subalternized, partially destroyed, and partially incorporated into the Spanish colonial exploitation of soil, subsoil, and human labor. The intricate network of kinship-based relations of barter that connected the diverse ecological zones of the Andean highlands and valleys were atomized and realigned in function of transatlantic interests. Although deprived of their reach and importance, vestiges of the reciprocal economy continue to survive: 'Andean peasants redirected agriculture toward commercial ends; engaged in trade and commerce; pursued artisanry and wage labor; mortgaged, sold and purchased lands; and sometimes even invested in the material and ideological trappings of European prestige' while simultaneously engaging in 'kinship based and barter reciprocities' (p. 19).

In view of the broader context of colonial economy in the Andes, Steve Stern similarly argued that – instead of an incorporation of indigenous economic forms into an expanding capitalist world-system – colonial economies exhibited diverse modes of production and exchange that do not fit into the categories of pre-capitalist, feudal, and capitalist economy. Thanks to the diverse strategies of negotiating with colonial power, indigenous agents modified their integration and thereby influenced the responses by colonial mercantile capitalists. The interaction between indigenous economic strategies and colonial forms of exploitation created thus a colonial mode of production characterized by diversity. This diversity, writes Stern, 'may speak not only to material uncertainties, opportunities, and contra-dictions particular to colonial life but also to distinctions in morality, ethos, and political culture that differentiated colony from metropolis' (Stern, 1988, p. 871).

The remains of such market economies, having survived on the border to global capitalism, are currently strengthened – along with traditional forms of governance and ethics – as indigenous media activists, indigenous intellectuals and historians work with their rural communities of origin (see Choque Quispe & Mamani Condori, 2003). As indigenous movements protest neoliberal policies, video makers partially disconnect video from capitalist production systems, from individual ownership and from commodification. The profit principal is not the guiding light for these communication processes, but this does not mean that all indigenous activists completely eschew the market. The Chiapas Media Project/Promedios in Mexico primarily networks Zapatista communities in Chiapas but partially funds its staff positions and hardware through sales to educational institutions, largely in the USA. They have taken advantage of the marketability of their videos in order to challenge common ideas about indigenous peoples and as a means of drawing international attention and support to the political and cultural struggle of the EZLN (Zapatista National Liberation Army). Others, such as CONAIE (Indigenous National Council of Ecuador) have assumed a flexible pricing policy for their films. Indigenous communities use CONAIE's archives for free or pay significantly less than others, such as US academics. In Ecuador the sale prices and availability of the videos depend on who is the buyer, and CONAIE has not made their films accessible through international distribution outlets or websites (Schiwy, 2009, chapter seven).

Indigenous video makers thus experiment with possibilities for transforming the rules of the market and maintaining a liminal space from which to think and act otherwise. When they seek to make their gaze part of national and international vision-scapes they certainly take advantage of the marketability of their videos (among indigenous communities world wide, social activists, and academics). However, this partial commodification cannot be reduced to acting upon a plane of immanence. As the logic of profit maximization is held in check, questioned and further disrupted through the rural circulation plans and integral production practices, indigenous media activists at least partially bypass the capitalist hegemonic market for cultural diversity. Enacting a reciprocal economy on screen and off points beyond the notion of development designed by western agencies (private or otherwise) who promote a greater share in wealth for indigenous populations. It also takes a different direction from socialist revolution. Even if the ethics of reciprocity resemble a communist ideal of shared wealth, affirming market relations and wealth and power differences within indigenous communities exceeds the socialist perspective on indigenous life. Instead these socio-economic relations resemble 'border thinking' where epistemological traditions that have been poised against each other in unequal ways through the colonial experience are brought to bear on each other, transcending eurocentrism (Mignolo, 2000, pp. 49–90). With respect to labor and market relations, indigenous media activists bring the global market for multicultural diversity in contact with reciprocal economy, subjecting the former to the economic ethics of the latter. From the perspective of indigenous media the global capitalist system is hence not characterized by an absence of colonial legacies or by immanence but rather structured by socio-economic borders that emerge from more than five hundred years of negotiating with capitalism.

Unless one sees colonial legacies as a structural continuity of capitalism, the notion of the multitude (agent of transformation) glosses over the uneven relationships of regions and subjectivities with each other and in relation to the hegemonic economic and epistemic order. If one agrees with the idea of the total capitalist permeation of life, or the subsumption of life to its regime, change is seen as immanent to its logic. However, biopower here also becomes amorphous. Upon closer examination the creative adaptations of indigenous rural communities have produced alternative spaces that are neither inside nor completely outside of the logic of capitalism. Virtual designs in turn have not shed their bodies but rather contribute to a postmodern reorganization of the coloniality of power (see Mignolo, 2002,

p. 228; Castro-Gómez, 2007, p. 429). Thinking from these perspectives may sharpen our understanding of where change indeed begins to occur.

Acknowledgements
I would like to thank the members of CEFREC (especially Iván Sanjinés and Reynaldo Yujra) and CAIB (particularly Julia Mosúa, Marcelina Cárdenas, Jesús Tapia, Marcelino Pinto and Alfredo Copa) for sharing their thoughts with me on several occasions since I first started research on indigenous media in 1999. Thanks to both organizations for allowing me to see many of their videos at their production center in La Paz, Bolivia throughout the years. Thanks as well to the National Museum of the American Indian who granted me access to their video collection. Translations are mine, unless otherwise noted.

Notes

1. For a selection of different positions see the essays in Kafka Zúñiga (2004). The strongest alternative proposal was issued by a coalition of multiple indigenous and peasant organizations. The document was printed on inexpensive paper and widely distributed for debate in rural and urban centers (*Asamblea*, 2006).
2. CSUTCB (Confederación Sindical Unica de Trabajadores Campesinos de Bolivia), CSCB (Confederacion Sindical de Colonizadores de Bolivia), the above mentioned CIDOB, CONAMAQ (Consejo Nacional de Ayllus y Markas del Qullasuyu), FNMCBBS (Federación Nacional de Mujeres Campesinas Indígenas Originarias de Bolivia Bartolina Sisa).
3. This position contrasts with the fruitful engagement of radical Italian philosophers by theorists and activists in Buenos Aires. See Colectivo Situaciones (2002) and Fontana et al. (2001).
4. The analysis of indigenous media productions in Bolivia, Ecuador and Colombia is based on my field research unless otherwise noted.
5. This tendency (still) contrasts with the way Australian Aborigines have creatively adapted documentary's and television's stylistic conventions as a means of talking back to the colonial gaze. Through parody, self-reflexivity, even avant-gardist aesthetics that mix realism and antirealism as well as poetic address (see Beattie, 2004, pp. 69–79) aboriginal film makers have at once made use of and undermined documentary's truth claims. Ten years prior to Beattie's account, Faye Ginsburg (1994, p. 368) noted that for most Australian Aboriginal video makers, form and innovative solutions do not seem relevant. The aesthetic criteria used by aboriginal people privilege instead the strengthening of community ties. As Beattie states, Aboriginal film makers have grown tired of documentary form and are moving into fiction where there seems to be greater space for creative reframing (2004, p. 66). Similarly, in Brazil, documentaries such as *Video nas Aldeias se Apresenta* reflexively and humorously address the relationship between indigenous video makers and the camera itself. For a more detailed discussion of indigenous documentaries made in Bolivia see Schiwy (2009, chapter five).
6. See also Shohat and Stam (1994) especially chapter 3. On the return of the gaze see also Rony (1996).
7. Alessandro Fornazzari discusses this aspect in depth in his essay in this volume.
8. The new global order, marked by networks, immaterial labor, and biopower is seen as coming into being as a response to the actions of labor movements, the emphasis on labor being stronger in Negri than in Hardt (Hardt & Negri, 2000, p. xii–xv, 8–9, 19; Negri, 2003).
9. I would like to thank Thomas Reese (Tulane University) for calling my attention to the pervasive representation of labor in CEFREC-CAIB's fiction videos.
10. Members of CAIB and CEFREC expressed these views in personal conversations as well as during discussions of their videos at international film and video festivals, for instance in Guatemala (1999) and New York (2000). See also Mosúa, Copa and Pinto (2000) and Flores (2001–02).

11. As CEFREC (2005, n.p.) sees it, the process of audiovisual communication strengthens the tradition of collective decision-making in the communities.

References

Aronowitz, S. (1979). Film: The art form of capitalism. *Social Text*, *1*, 110–129.

Asamblea Nacional de Organizaciones Indigenas, Originarias, Campesinas y de Colonizadores de Bolivia (2006). *Propuesta para la nueva constitutición política del estado*. Sucre: Asamblea Nacional.

Bazin, A. (1974). *What is cinema?* Comp. and trans. H. Gray. Berkeley, Los Angeles & London: University of California Press.

Beattie, K. (2004). *Documentary screens. Nonfiction film and television*. New York: Palgrave MacMillan.

Castro-Gómez, S. (2007). The missing chapter of empire: Postmodern reorganization of coloniality and post-Fordist capitalism. *Cultural Studies*, *21*(2–3), 428–448.

CEFREC. (2005). Communication strategies and indigenous rights. Report on the indigenous aboriginal national plan for audiovisual communication, 2000–2004. Trans. F. Schiwy. Unpublished Grant Report, n.p.

Choque Quispe, M.E., & Mamani Condori, C. (2003). Reconstitución del ayllu y derechos de los pueblos indígenas: El movimiento indígena en los Andes de Bolivia. In E. Ticona Alejo (Ed.), *Los Andes desde Los Andes. Aymaranakana, Qhichwanakana, yatxatawipa, Lup'iwipa* (pp. 147–170). La Paz: Yachaywasi.

Colectivo Situaciones (2002). *19 y 20. Apuntes para el nuevo protagonismo social*. Buenos Aires: Ediciones de Mano en Mano.

Escobar, A. (2007). Worlds and knowledges otherwise: The Latin American modernity/coloniality research program. *Cultural Studies*, *21*(2–3), 179–210.

Flores, D. (2001). Bolivian links. Indigenous media. Interview with Julia Mosúa, Alfredo Copa & Marcelino Pinto. Transcr. by F. Schiwy, trans. S. Briante. *Bomb*, *78*, 30–35.

Fontana, E., Fontana, N., Gago, V., Santucho, M., Scolnik, S., & Sztulwark, D. (2001). *Contrapoder. Una introducción*. Buenos Aires: Ediciones de Mano en Mano.

Ginsburg, F. (1994). Embedded aesthetics: Creating a discursive space for indigenous media. *Cultural Anthropology*, *9*(3), 365–382.

Haraway, D.J. (1997). *Modest_Witness@Second_Millennium. FemaleMan©_Meets_Onco-Mouse™*. New York: Routledge.

Hardt, M., & Negri, A. (2000). *Empire*. Cambridge: Harvard University Press.

Hayles, N.K. (1999). *How we became posthuman. Virtual bodies in cybernetics, literature, and informatics*. Chicago: University of Chicago Press.

Hayles, N.K. (2005). *My mother was a computer. Digital subjects and literary texts*. Chicago: University of Chicago Press.

Himpele, J. (2004). Packaging indigenous media: An interview with Ivan Sanjinés & Jesús Tapia. *American Anthropologist*, *106*(2), 354–363.

Jameson, F. (2000). *The cultural turn. Selected writings on the postmodern 1983–1998*. London & New York: Verso.

Kafka Zúñiga, J. (Ed.). (2004). *Asamblea constituyente. Hacia un nuevo estado Boliviano*. La Paz: Colegio de politólogos, Universidad Católica Boliviana, Comisión Episcopal Pastoral Social (Caritas).

Kaplan, E.A. (1997). *Looking for the other. Feminism, film, and the imperial gaze*. New York: Routledge.

Larson, B. (1995). Andean communities, political cultures, and markets: The changing contours of a field. In B. Larson & O. Harris (Eds.) with E. Tandeter, *Ethnicities and markets in the Andes* (pp. 5–53). Durham: Duke University Press.

Lazzarato, M. (1996). Immaterial labor. In P. Virno (Ed.), & M. Hardt *Radical thought in Italy. A potential politics* (pp. 132–146). *Theory out of bounds* 7. Minneapolis & London: University of Minnesota Press.

Mamani Ramírez, P. (2006). Dominación étnica, de clase y territorialización del poder indígena en Bolivia. In R. Gutiérrez & F. Escárzaga (Eds.), *Movimiento indígena en América Latina: resistencia y proyecto alternativo* (Vol. 2, pp. 35–53). Mexico: Casa Juan Pablos;

Centro de Estudios Andinos y Mesoamericanos; Benemérita Universidad Autónoma de Puebla.

Mignolo, W.D. (2000). *Local histories/global designs. Coloniality, subaltern knowledges and border thinking*. Princeton Studies in Culture/Power/History, Princeton: Princeton University Press.

Mignolo, W.D. (2002). Colonialidad global, capitalismo y hegemonía epistémica. In C. Walsh, F. Schiwy, & S. Castro-Gómez (Eds.), *Indisciplinar las ciencias sociales. Geopolíticas del conocimiento y colonialidad del poder. Perspectivas desde lo andino* (pp. 227–234). Quito: UASB; Ediciones Abya-Yala.

Miller, T., Govil, N., McMurria, J., Maxwell, R., & Wang, T. (2005). *Global Hollywood 2*. London: BFI.

Mosúa, J., Copa, A., & Pinto, M. (2000). *Entrevista. Entrevista con Daniel Flores* [Audiorec.]. Transcribed by F. Schiwy. International Indigenous Film and Video Festival, New York.

Murra, J.V. (2002). *El mundo Andino. Población, medio ambiente y economía*. Lima: Pontificia Universidad Católica del Perú, Fondo Editorial; IEP.

Negri, A. (2003). Toni Negri en Buenos Aires. In A. Negri, G. Cocco, C. Altamira, & A. Horowicz. (Eds.), *Diálogo sobre la globalización, la multitud y la experiencia artentina. Espacios del Saber* 35 (pp. 25–50). Buenos Aires: Paidós.

Poster, M. (2006). *Information please. Culture and politics in the age of digital media*. Durham: Duke University Press.

Quijano, A., & Wallerstein., I. (1992). Americanity as a concept, or the Americas in the modern world-system. *ISSI*, *134*, 549–557.

Reich, R.B. (2007). *Supercapitalism. The transformation of business, democracy, and every day life*. New York: Alfred A. Knopf.

Rivera Cusicanqui, S. (1996). Trabajo de Mujeres: Explotación capitalista y opresión colonial entre las migrantes aymaras de La Paz y El Alto, Bolivia. In S. Rivera Cusicanqui (Ed.), *Ser mujer indígena, chola o birlocha en la Bolivia postcolonial de los años 90* (pp. 163–300). La Paz: Ministerio de Desarrollo Humano, Secretaría de Asuntos Etnicos, de Género y Generacionales, Subsecretaría de Asuntos de Género.

Rodowick, D.N. (2001). Dr. Strange Media; or, How I learned to stop worrying and love film theory. *PMLA*, *116*(5), 1396–404.

Rony, F.T. (1996). *The third eye. Race, cinema, and ethnographic spectacle*. Durham: Duke University Press.

Schiwy, F. (2007). Decolonization and the question of subjectivity: Gender, race, and binary thinking. *Cultural Studies*, *21*(2–3), 271–294.

Schiwy, F. (2009). *Indianizing film. Decolonization, the Andes, and the question of technology*. Newark: Rutgers UP.

Shohat, E., & Stam, R. (1994). *Unthinking Eurocentrism. Multiculturalism and the media*. New York: Routledge.

Sinclair, J., & Turner, G. (Eds.). (2004). *Contemporary world television*. London: BFI.

Stephenson, M. (2002). Forging an indigenous counterpublic sphere: The taller de historia oral Andina in Bolivia. *Latin American Research Review*, *37*(2), 99–118.

Stern, S.J. (1988). Feudalism, capitalism, and the world-system in the perspective of Latin America and the Caribbean. *The American Historical Review*, *93*(4), 829–72.

Virno, P. (2005). Virtuosity and revolution: The political theory of exodus. Retrieved 17 October 2005 from http://www.generaton-online.org/c/fcmultitude2.html

Filmography

Cárdenas, M. (*Responsable*). (2001). *Llanthupi munakuy/Loving each other in the shadows* [Fiction, in Quechua with English subtitles]. Bolivia: CEFREC-CAIB.

Cárdenas, M. (*Responsable*). (2005). *Rebeldías y esperanzas/Rebellions and hopes* [Documentary, in Spanish]. Bolivia: CEFREC-CAIB.

Carelli, V., & Correa, M. (Directors). (2002). *Video nas aldeias se apresenta/Video in the villages presents itself* [Documentary, with English subtitles]. Brazil: Video nas aldeias.

CEFREC-CAIB (2000). *Los pueblos indígenas así pensamos/Indigenous peoples, this is how we think* [Digital video recording, in various languages with Spanish or English subtitles]. Bolivia: CEFREC-CAIB.

CEFREC-CAIB (2005). *Rumbo a la Asamblea Constituyente. Conociendo nuestros derechos impulsamos nuestras propuestas. Estrategia nacional de comunicación derechos indígenas y originarios hacia la Asamblea Constituyente.* [Multimedia package]. Bolivia: CEFREC-CAIB.

Copa, A. (*Responsable*). (1999). *Desempolvando nuestra historia* [Docufiction, in Quechua and Spanish]. Bolivia: CEFREC-CAIB.

Gibson, M. (Director). (2006). *Apocalypto* [Fiction, in Yucatec Maya with English subtitles]. USA: Touchstone Pictures.

Jackson, P. (Director). (2005). *King Kong* [Fiction]. New Zealand and USA: Universal Studios.

Luna, P. (*Responsable*). (1998). *Qulqi chaliku. El chaleco de plata/The silver vest* [Fiction, in Aymara with Spanish subtitles and Spanish]. Bolivia: CEFREC-CAIB.

Mosúa, J. (*Responsable*). (1999). *Nuestra palabra. La historia de San Francisco de Moxos* [Docufiction, in Moxeño with Spanish voiceover and Spanish]. Bolivia: CEFREC-CAIB.

Peña, F. (*Responsable*). (1999). *Espíritu de la selva, el/The forest spirit* [Digital video recording, in Spanish]. Bolivia: CEFREC-CAIB.

Pinto, M. (*Responsable*). (1999). *El oro maldito/Cursed gold* [Fiction, in Quechua with Spanish Subtitles and Spanish]. Bolivia: CEFREC-CAIB.

Yujra, R. (*Responsable*). (1999). *Qati qati. Susurros de muerte/Whispers of death* [Fiction, in Aymara with Spanish subtitles]. Bolivia: CEFREC-CAIB.

Yujra, R. (*Responsable*). (2003). *K'anchariy/Para encender la luz del espíritu* [Documentary, digital video recording]. Bolivia: CEFREC-CAIB.

Capital implications: the function of labor in the video art of Juan Devis and Yoshua Okón

Kenneth Rogers

Department of Media and Cultural Studies, University of California, Riverside, USA

It is increasingly evident that advanced forms of speculative value that have become the driving engine behind the inflated global art market are nonetheless inextricably bound to and dependent upon more informal market systems that operate through the spontaneous organization of exploitable, precarious, marginalized, and ultimately undervalued forms of labor. This fact makes labor a pivotal site where the linkages between these two purportedly independent markets (and their respective systems of value and exchange) come into focus and can be more tangibly assessed and critiqued. This paper will follow this current by first contextualizing the function of labor within two contrasting historical traditions/tendencies of art and cultural production that explicitly reference labor as an essential structuring condition of the work. It will then develop a detailed case study of a recent exchange between two contemporary media/video artists in Los Angeles that demonstrates the complexities of how the market value of art is implicated within a precarious trans-national wage labor system in the neoliberalist global economy.

In a surprising stylistic departure for an artist committed to grassroots aesthetics, a recent video by media activist Juan Devis is a high-end television pilot produced for mainstream broadcast or satellite distribution. *Inter-State: Video on the Go* (2004) is a sleek hybrid format somewhere between reality television and behind-the-scenes documentary that follows three separate Los Angeles-based studio artists each through the production of a single work of art, from conception to realization. Although the piece works through themes and issues common to Devis' media activist, theater, and experimental film background, the format stands in dramatic contrast to these earlier efforts by featuring markedly more commercial conventions: rapid editing, sensational visuals, a polished soundtrack and score, traditional narrative arc, youth culture appeal, and brief digestible segments conveniently divided for commercial interruption – in short, the requisite ingredients necessary for transforming the social document into entertainment. This stands in contrast to nearly all of Devis' earlier work: an avant-garde adaptation of a short story by Clarice Lispector, *The Petty Curse of Having this Body* (1993); an austere testimonial video documentary on the politics of AIDS in his native Colombia, *Hielo* (1996); a found-footage meditation on populist leader Jorge Gaitán's early political speeches in the Plaza Bolivar in Bogotá, *La Calle del Pecado Mortal* (1998); a myriad of non-profit, community-based youth media projects, *Face-In* (2000), *The Belmont Tunnel* (2002), *Tropical America* (2003); and a documentary involving five families' organizational struggle in the development of a migrant workers' union, *The Digital Migrant* (in progress).

But the choice of format does not passively conform to the demands of market forces; it also tactically inserts an alternative sensibility into this mainstream format. The video first premiered at the Redcat Theater in November 2004 as part of LA Freewaves, a biennial, a non-profit independent media festival and a major venue for the exhibition and distribution of alternative film and video in Los Angeles. More importantly, the video was the first work ever funded and produced *by* Freewaves, and stands as a kind of showcase of a new way for the non-profit to connect to a broader cultural sphere beyond the art-going cognoscenti of Southern California. Thus *Inter-State* signals a shift that is not only relevant to the *oeuvre* of a single artist, but also signals a new approach to alternative media distribution that no longer adheres to the clean dichotomy between dominant commercial production and its alternatives by constantly exploring ways of bringing one sphere of media praxis to bear on the other. In what might arguably appear as a problematic acquiescence to the imperatives of the market, there exists a buried critique of the political economy of commercial television by subtly implicating it within a much broader array of social practices, cultures, and economies that are customarily excluded from reference within that system, or if they do appear, are appropriated into a palliative form of mass consumption – a form that does not endanger the hegemony of neoliberalist, free-market interests. So despite its commercial appeal, one still finds in *Inter-State* all the same themes, which deal with issues of class and power, threaded throughout so much of Devis' activist work; the culture of the automobile; Latin American identity politics; issues of migration, trans-nationalism, and diaspora experience; Border Art and Southland culture; and political economy and labor politics. *Inter-State* is a curious experiment, pushing a more progressive and activist agenda into a commercial container to discover if its local community advocacy can still resonate within a mainstream cultural economy.

This marriage between activism and commerce, however, is not always a happy one, and it brings numerous internal contradictions and tensions to the surface of the work, primarily the problem of whether the video has compromised its ability to deliver real agency to the expanded community it seeks. In addressing a mainstream audience through a mainstream format, the question becomes whether or not *Inter-State* achieves an adequate retention of an activist sensibility or slides into a state of complicity with a mode of production and distribution that is inimical to its own ethos by implicating itself within a form of dominant media grounded in free-market capitalism. Just as it inserts moments of resistance into this dominant cultural form, the piece also struggles in its ability to open a truly participatory, non-hierarchical, and interactive space and often reverts to a voice that speaks for rather than from the groups and subjects who are institutionally excluded from access to these forms of culture. At the same time, it also critiques a certain grassroots naiveté invested in the possibility of any truly participatory, non-hierarchical form of culture not conscripted by power relationships and defined by global capital. In this sense, *Inter-State* is a complex and self-contradictory video. Suspended between competing institutional demands and deeply ambivalent in its mode of address, it is a work that demonstrates the polysemy of its title in a composite tension between its social aesthetic and its mode of production.

It is in and around the issue of labor politics that *Inter-State* explicitly plays out the internal tension between its alternative, grassroots aspirations and the political economy of mainstream television. The struggle over the depiction of labor becomes absolutely central to both the video's content and, more importantly, its relations of production. *Inter-State* documents three Latino, Southern Californian artists whose work straddles both the upper stratum of the contemporary art world and informal, less institutionalized cultures and economies external to that world. The first is devoted to Rubén Ortiz-Torres' *La Zamba del Chevy* (2000), in which Ortiz-Torres collaborates with car artist Tony Ortiz to convert a replica of Che Guevara's 1960 Chevy Biscayne into a low-rider for a 3-D film and dancing car performance at the Getty Center; the second documents the evolution of Rubén Ochoa's *Class: C* (ongoing), a mobile art gallery created from a hand-me-down van formerly used as a tortilla delivery vehicle by his father; and the final segment documents the production of Yoshua Okón's *Shoot* (2004) a re-enactment of a generic Hollywood shootout made by hiring day-laborers as actors that debuted at The Project, Los Angeles in October 2004. In terms of content, all three segments depict artists whose work extends beyond the white walls of the museum and gallery system to the broader context of class struggle and labor relations in Southern California, but it is only within the final segment – a complex exchange between Okón and Devis – that this depiction turns structurally inward to confront the dilemma of how to indicate the function of labor within the productive forces of the video itself. In much the same way the video walks a line between grassroots and commercial aesthetics, the Okón segment develops a manner of performing the labor of cultural production so as to make a limited, local intervention against the advancement of capital while remaining implicated within capital, rather than aspiring to the unattainable task of standing outside it. I believe this exchange to be exemplary of the challenges and the new possibilities of bringing the issue of labor to the surface of cultural production at a moment when the social, material, political, and economic conditions that constitute what labor is, where it occurs, and how it produces value have been undergoing an epistemological transformation within the biopolitical context.

The Devis/Okón segment of *Inter-State* grapples with what I view as two contrasting traditions of the representation of labor in socially engaged art. So before delving further into the details of their co-production, it is crucial to first place their work within this context. The first and most straightforward way in which labor comes to the surface of the work is in the figuration of the laboring body – a practice that has its own place in the history of the plastic arts, but also in photography, literature, performance, radio, cinema, etc. In this simple form of bringing labor forward, a particular instance of labor is depicted by the work, and the work stands in for, refers to, and frames a specific historical condition of labor that is external to the work itself, often with the ethical intent of raising political consciousness about the inequitable conditions of that labor by making those conditions visible. This form of bringing labor to the surface of the work might be referred to as the *representational axis* of labor, in that the work points to or serves as an expression of labor that presumably exists in a world that is external to that work.

Toward the end of the nineteenth century, the representational depiction of industrial labor in realist painting was taken up by a new form of social documentary that migrated to the medium of photography due to technological advancements and the rising evidentiary import of the photograph as an arbiter of truth, both of which were connected to the growing bureaucratic and disciplinary needs of the state (Sekula, 1992; Tagg, 1993). Jacob Riis' 1890 social critique of the New York tenements, *How the Other Half Lives*, was pivotal in establishing this new photographic genre, perhaps most notably taken up two decades later in Lewis Hine's iconic photo essays on child labor made between 1908–12, which were accompanied by photo captions stressing social justice for the brutal exploitation of the immigrant underclass. After Hine, the photojournalistic tradition has held a privileged place in the representation of labor throughout twentieth century visual culture; however, in the terms I have put forward the representational axis is a category that cuts across historical periods, genre, and medium. Thus works as diverse as the Social Realist murals of Orozco or Rivera, Luchino Visconti's *la terra trema*, Barbara Kopple's *Harlan County*, and Sebastião Salgado's workers series might all be considered works that reference labor along the representational axis.

But there is a second, more indirect way in which labor comes to the surface of the work. It can also appear through the infolding of systems and procedures in and around the work that reveal how labor manifests as a precondition of that work's place within a broader economy. In this more complex form, the visible depiction of labor is secondary to its presence in the work as a kind of placeholder, abstraction, and potentiality. Labor is primarily referenced as an essential mechanism that posits art and culture's *potential* circulation as exchange value; and it often does so with the intent of demystifying the complex constructions upon which that value is based. This second form might be called the *functional axis* of labor, in that the work reflexively indicates its own function within a larger system of relations, a system that is entirely dependent upon the abstract potential of empty labor for it to operate.

The functional axis of labor became ever more prevalent during the 1960s when a global paradigm shift in art practice turned to duration, performance, demater-ialization, the blurring of art/life dichotomies, and institutional critiques as multi-layered strategies for disrupting the commodification of art (Rorimer, 2001; Sekula, 1978; Wall, 1995). Of the many the tactics indicating the function of labor, such as the use of timetables and graphs, indexical references to the context of exhibition and circulation, and documents or plans that refer to process and construction, the most common to the United States context were found in the many works in which artists used their own bodies and actions as a way of demonstrating the intersection of art labor with that of other economies. Bonnie Sherk's performance piece *Act V, Andy's Donuts*, when she took a job as a short order cook for the overnight shift in a San Francisco diner between June 1973 and May 1974, and Mierle Ukeles performance *Washing Tracks Maintenance* (1973), in which she attended to the daily upkeep of the Wadsworth museum by sweeping, cleaning, and scrubbing the exhibition space for the duration of a group show are two such examples of work that indicates the complex function of exchange value by oppositionally overlaying one economic system of evaluation with another, in which privileged artist labor is equated with undervalued wage labor (see Figure 1). Similarly, in one of his five one-year endurance performances made between 1978–86, *Time Clock*, Tehching Hsieh punched a time clock in his studio every hour on the hour, 24 hours a day, seven

Figure 1. Mierle Laderman Ukeles *Washing, Tracks, Maintenance*, Wadsworth Museum (1973). Courtesy Ronald Feldman Fine Arts, New York.

days a week, for the duration of one year (Foley, 1981). Through the extended duration of the piece, this consuming performance strips bare the naked brutality of the workweek and the imprint and adjustments endured by the modern subject who must synchronize with the indifferent rhythms of capital. But the functional axis is present in scores of other artworks where the actions of an artist's body become the work (or substrate for the work) and deliver a more implicit critique by impeding institutional criteria accustomed to reading artist labor as a material quality in objects, legible as form and style. In the performance works of Eleanor Antin, Bruce Nauman, Chris Burden, Joan Jonas, Vito Acconci, Carolee Schneemann, et al., the immaterial, durational actions of their bodies, not the physical traces that remain, become the work (O'Dell, 2000). In this way, much of the art of this period is not only about its own labor, but is actually biopolitically undifferentiated from the labor expended to produce it, irregardless of the material residue it leaves behind.

It can be said that there is an important variant on the functional axis of labor that is common within, but not exclusive to Latin American Conceptual Art. Although similarly directed at issues of exploitation and the inequitable distribution of wealth, the tendency of the social critique of labor in US Conceptual Art, performance, etc. was to emphasize the individual body of the artist or performer as labor rather than engage with labor in those exploited communities. In the US and Western European context, the politics of labor was often individuated; the travail of the artist was his or her own but little more than a metaphor vis-à-vis the broader social field. By contrast, the tendency in Latin American more often avoids the individualist approach preferring more direct contact with the laborer in the broader social field. In what still stands as the most emblematic example of this approach, in 1968 Argentinian artist Oscar Bony paid a working family double their customary wages to sit atop a podium on display for the duration of an exhibition. Bony made his comment on labor's unremarked function in art not through a performance of his own, but through the remuneration of others hired to perform the labor that is later attributed to him. In doing so he references the disengagement and hypocrisy of institutional systems blind to external economic conditions and class disparity. The haunting objectification of the working family also betrays a formal system of property rights, as the ownership a work produced by wage labor is attributed to Bony's namesake. The piece is also an indictment against the inherent violence imbedded in any claim to representational authenticity by implying that the representational axis always objectifies and consumes the lives of those it claims to present. Here the labor of the artist is not a kind of functional poetics that devalues the currency of art, but the artist's class privilege is placed firmly on the table for contemplation, along with the racial codifications that reinforce such a disparity (Ramírez, 1999).

This approach toward the functional axis remained operative in the 1990s when Spanish artist Santiago Sierra, working in Mexico, Peru, Cuba, and Brazil, made a series of remuneration pieces in the tradition of Bony, in which he hired local workers to perform actions that would become art. Sierra is a brazenly extreme case study of this later tradition and from the 1990s forward he has hired individuals from the deprived underclasses to engage in menial, demeaning, and exploitative actions to produce his work. Hiring migrant workers, the unemployed, sex workers and day-laborers at wages slightly above market rate, he has produced numerous remuneration pieces. In Mexico City, he remunerated workers to detach and manually maintain support of a gallery wall at a 60-degree angle for the duration of the piece; paid a worker to remain in the trunk of a car for an extended period; paid Cuban sex workers to be covered by wooden boxes used as benches for an art opening; and paid a shoe shine boy to clean the shoes of privileged patrons attending an art opening. He has also paid subjects to mark their bodies with tattoos or hair dye and has even seemingly put their health at risk by covering remunerated persons with plastic and spraying them with polyurethane (see Figure 2).

As might be expected, pointed criticisms of Sierra's works' undeniably exploitative dimension have been repeatedly voiced. For creating works that are worth exponentially more the than the wages paid to produce them as well as for the inherently degrading and pointless nature of the performances themselves, he is often criticized for being an unrepentant opportunist leveraging neo-colonialist cultural and class privilege to secure a position as an international art star. The contrary position is that Sierra is simply making explicit reference to what most cultural producers disavow, suggesting that it is an artist's obligation to own up to that accountability. As Coco Fusco suggests, Sierra,

Figure 2.   Santiago Sierra. *The Wall of a Gallery Pulled Out, Inclined 60 Degrees from the Ground and Sustained by 5 People.* Acceso A. Mexico City, Mexico. April 2000. Courtesy of the artist and Lisson Gallery.

foregrounds desperation and futility, the gap between rich and poor, the constant humiliation to which the needy are subjected, and the discretionary power of those with even a modicum of wealth. His performances suggest a view of contemporary Mexican society clinging to the hierarchies established under Spanish rule. (2001, p. 67)

Although they should not be compared in any deterministic way or as an absolute correlation, the contrast between representational and functional axes might be said to loosely correspond to Marx's distinction between uncapitalized craft labor and capitalized abstract labor: between labor that has not yet entered into a condition of absolute exchangeability because its value is the value of a particular task and labor that has been rendered as potential for capital exploitation because of its interchangeability. When capital asserts itself as an arbiter between all particular forms of labor, it converts that particularity into abstract use value for capital known as labor-power. Marx writes:

[L]abour is of course in each single case a specific labour, but capital can come into relation with every *specific* labour; it confronts the *totality* of all labours [potentiality], and the particular one it confronts at a given time is an accidental matter. On the other side, the worker himself is absolutely indifferent to the specificity of his labour; it has no interest for him as such, but only in as much as it is in fact *labour* and, as such, a use value for capital. It is therefore his economic character that he is the carrier of labour as such – i.e. of labour as *use value* for capital; he is a worker, in opposition to the capitalist. This is not the character of the craftsmen and guild-members. (1973, pp. 296–97)

It seems to me that even the most naked representation of industrial labor along the representational axis corresponds to Marx's nostalgic conception of pre-capitalized craft labor because the epistemology of its aesthetic base is grounded in the specificity of that representation. Alternatively, works that emphasize the functional axis loosely correspond to capitalized labor in that they don't represent, but rather perform the abstract condition that makes that exploitation possible: the intercession of capital. So although I observe Marx's distinction of labor in my construction of these two terms, I also try to show how the representational and the functional are less fixed in absolute opposition and always interpenetrate to some degree. In addition, it is important to allow the two terms to relate simultaneously to Marx's more orthodox view of value in the political economy (i.e., value measured by the extraction of surplus value by capital) and simultaneously open a space to account for the realm of biopolitical production and the new forms of value endemic to it (i.e., value immanent to the social field), forms that facilitate the movement between asset capital and cultural capital, political economy and social economy, money and/as art.

That said, it becomes important to note that the functional axis does not exclude the representational, as it is most often the case that the terms always correlate. The reference to the functional axis of labor is often achieved through a delicate balance of interdependent relationships, such as social context, site, history, mode of exhibition and distribution, etc. Because many of these contingencies include representational aspects, reference to the function of labor is always an unstable proposition, often making it a merely temporary intervention that is forever on the verge of collapse back onto the representational axis. Likewise, every representational work potentially contains a functional aspect that might be revealed through a process of strategic re-contextualization, like placing the classical work on an epistemological auction block (Sherri Levine's *After Walker Evans* (1981) series comes to mind as an example of such re-contextualization). Furthermore, it is often the forces of institutional re-appropriation that convert the functional back into the representational, because it is a common reflex for cultural institutions to efface their own implication in the economy made visible by the functional axis, or to at least territorialize it within the boundary of 'subversive' culture – thus dada becomes 'Dada' and the durational labor of Ukeles' *Washing, Tracks, Maintenance* performance becomes an exhibition one-liner synecdochally condensed into a single photograph. This is all to suggest that these two terms do not sit in absolute opposition but often coexist, work in tandem, form offshoots of one another, and constantly work to transform each other. This process is ongoing but also asymmetrical, as it is usually the case that the functional axis depends upon or branches out of the representational, but that the representational axis seeks to negate, disavow, or reabsorb the functional as it has difficulty coexisting peaceably alongside of it.

By the time Sierra was working in Mexico City it was within an entirely different economic paradigm from that of Bony. The global art market that found representations of labor so fashionable – along with the late-capitalist museum (Krauss, 1990) that now collect and exhibit them – emerged out of neoliberalist reforms that mark the Reaganite and Thatcherite revolutions of the 1980s. This wave of reform began profoundly to reshape global trade through policies and institutions that fostered both national and international deregulation. From the privatization of everything from public works to prison systems, the measured excision of state oversight and control has been conjoined with a systematic rollback of expenditure for social services. A myriad of major multilateral and bilateral trade agreements were then established: NAFTA (1994) and MAI (1995–1998) have reduced tariffs and facilitated the unchecked flow of capital across national borders; GATT's formation of the WTO in 1994 has since made it the dominant supranational institution that dictates global economic policy; and the last vestiges of Keynesianism have been squeezed out of the IMF and the World Bank, which have now become the global strong-arm to convert the world's poorer national economies to the neoliberalist agenda. Overall, this wave of neoliberalist reform has meant a diminishment of state sovereignty. Seeking to open new channels for the flow of capital that were previously limited by nationalist protectionism, the state has become an agent of multinational corporations, as one can easily glean from the ominously sequestered G8 summits. All this is happening under the ambiguous, divisive designation known as globalization (Harvey, 2005; Hardt & Negri, 2004).

But there is perhaps no greater material effect of globalization than its impact upon labor worldwide. Relinquished of their responsibilities to national trade unions, multinational corporations have been transferring manufacturing and outsourcing the service sector to the exploited and vulnerable labor forces of China and India. The 'free' trade of NAFTA has devastated the Mexican working class, particularly agricultural workers, who have crossed the US border to work as migrant farmers, day-laborers, and in sweatshops. With the influx of inexpensive goods from China to the US economy and the fragmentation of trade unions, better-paying skilled manufacturing jobs have been transferred to the low-wage, precarious service sector, where franchise box stores like Walmart and Home Depot flood the market with discounted bulk goods that crush local retailers.

Okón is working in the same tradition as artists like Bony, Sierra, and Alÿs, and was a contemporary of Sierra and Alÿs in the post-NAFTA period of Mexican Contemporary art. Co-founder of La Panadería (1994–2002), a non-profit, artist-run international exhibition space and cultural center in Mexico City, Okón began his career at a moment when the deregulated flow of capital and labor across the Mexican border forced a downward wage pressure that began to erode locally-based industry. Symbolically occupying the shell of a former bakery in La Condesa, a gentrifying neighborhood within Mexico City, La Panadería became the epicenter of experimental art and performance that was critically engaged with the cultural and economic transformations of the new global trade policies and paradigms that were reshaping Mexican culture and commerce. Okón's own works from this period approach the functional axis through monetary transactions between himself and a participant that reveal socially and economically-determined power relationships. In works like *A Propósito* (1997), an installation that includes a gross of black market car stereos alongside a video of an accomplished thief ransacking cars to acquire them, and *Orillese a la Orilla* (1999–2000), a nine-part video series in which the artist solicits performances from the Mexican police – often with bribes – that compromise their authority and at times their dignity, one can see the influence of the experimental Panadería years upon his more recent work. These transactions often reveal unanticipated moral ambiguities. In the fifth tableau of *Orillese a la Orilla* (1999–2000), for example, Okón pays a police officer to do a square dance, a piece that inevitably elicits mixed responses. By one measure, Okón's piece raises the issue of the officer's subordinated position within Mexican class and racial hierarchies and how these inequities permit a perceived exploitation of the officer by Okón himself. From another side however, the piece confers a kind of suspicion upon the potential corruption of representatives of state power, making the social critique that, for the right price, any authority might be bought or sold, made to dance to any tune. Still another reading is that Okón's gesture is not at all exploitative but opens a space of performative transgression for an individual unwillingly caught in the stricture of a particular social role. Gesturing toward moral ambiguities such as these is typical of Okón's projects (Debroise, 2006; Dorfsman, 2005).

Okón, now based in Los Angeles, is producing work that is similar in tactics but relevant to the very different social and political landscape of the California Southland, and it was in this different environment that the collaboration with Devis took place. The Devis/Okón project[1] perpetually seeks and approaches the functional axis of labor by producing within itself a complex kind of auto-referential economy that mirrors and parallels but also literally connects to other economies external to it. It not only represents labor, but also refers to labor as an abstract precondition of its own value, a value that determines the project's superfluidity within various institutional and cultural circuits. In this sense, their project maintains continuity with the increased skepticism toward the representational axis that appeared in the late-1960s, but, alternatively, it underscores the difficulty in making a sustained critique of labor in this way, as it is a project that does not exempt itself from the way in which a reference to labor's function works in complicity with structures that re-appropriate the functional back into the representational. In the analysis that follows, I wish to examine the place between *Inter-State* and *Shoot* where this tension, in all of its permutations, is most fraught and therefore most visible in the work.

To better unpack the complexities of how the collaboration between Devis and Okón works toward the functional representation of labor, it is necessary to work forward from Okón's installation into the multiple levels of auto-referentiality and intertextual exchange that make *Shoot* and *Inter-State* indistinguishable from one another. The armature for this exchange is structured out of Okón's video installation *Shoot*, which explores the foggy boundary between cinematic fiction and documentary fact, and how the two categories are ceaselessly regenerating one another, an issue especially pertinent to the cultural media nexus of Los Angeles. He structured his own piece out of the intertextual exchange around a violent, live-broadcast news event, a bank robbery in 1997 known as the North Hollywood shootout. An event in which two masked gunmen with automatic weapons robbed a bank and shot indiscriminately at bystanders and police, the North Hollywood shootout was already a copycat crime of a fictional event, as it was later discovered the bank robbery scene in Michael Mann's *Heat* (1995) inspired the gunmen. Upon discovering that the 'real' robbery had then subsequently inspired yet another fictional Hollywood production, *44 Minutes: The North Hollywood Shootout* (2003), Okón sought his own continuation of the intertextual relay and produced a low-budget, guerilla-style rendition of the scene. After acquiring a demolished police car from a junkyard, he cast the roles of seven police officers by auditioning migrant day-laborers outside of a Home Depot, where undocumented workers in Southern California customarily hustle for day jobs. Once the casting selections had been made, the actors, without costumes or stage props other than the police car, pantomimed a scene of their being assailed and massacred by two gunmen who metaphorically occupied the place of the two cameras documenting the performance (one of which was operated by Devis). The final gallery presentation consisted of a synchronized, two-channel video projection above the police car that sat vacant beneath like an artifact from the scene of a crime (see Figure 3).

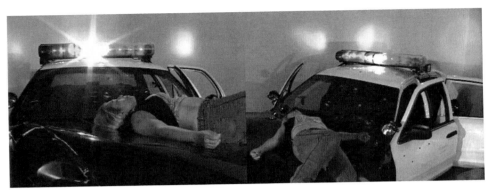

Figure 3.   Yoshua Okón. *Shoot*. Los Angeles, 2004. Courtesy of the artist and The Project, NY.

The functional axis is not fully revealed in either Devis or Okón's piece, but in the interstice between the two, which becomes visible when one reads the complex intertext between *Shoot* and *Inter-State* as a single project, a semi-autonomous realm that opens a spiral of co-implicated exchange. This exchange begins perhaps with Devis tactically inserting himself into the production of Okón's *Shoot*. Of the three segments in *Inter-State*, it is only within the Okón segment, subtitled *245 (d) 1: Assault with Firearm Upon a Police Officer*, that the presence of Devis as documentarian is outwardly textualized. It is the only segment in which Devis himself reflexively appears in the film behind the camera, in which his voice is audibly included when asking interviewees questions and giving directives, and in which he explicitly editorializes, critiques, and reshapes the artist's piece as it might otherwise stand alone in the gallery. All this is not to suggest that *245 (d) 1* is any less authentic than the Ortiz-Torres and Ochoa segments, but simply that it represents a marked shift in the video's mode of address by bringing forward its maker as a participant in the very thing he sets out to document. Linked to the highly reflexive nature of *Shoot* itself, Devis' reflexivity toward his own process replicates the power dynamic between Okón and his actors.

Much of this exchange orbits around to the issue of labor. By following *Shoot* from conception to exhibition, *245 (d) 1* is the only segment of the series that documents not just the work of art, but also the labor expended in the production of that work. It tracks the laboring artist as he selects a demolished police car, auditions and directs actors, prepares the set at The Project, and shoots *Shoot*. But what governs the causal progression of these scenes of physical labor is the construction of Okón as the orchestrator of the process. It is invariably a voice-over or talking-head interview of Okón elaborating on the motivations of his process, the conceptual and theoretical registers of the piece, and his general philosophy of art that animates the sequence that demonstrates their realization. By placing Okón at the elocutionary center of the segment, whose thoughts and words drive the shoot forward, Devis' *245 (d) 1* interrogates a system that places immaterial/intellectual labor in a supervising or managerial role over the subordinate material/physical labor. Yet as much as the documentary segment exposes Okón's labor as management, it equally esteems his labor as artist, having recourse to the myth of the expressive independence of artistic labor from the external interests of capital – the myth of art as an expressive form that originates from the creative autonomy of the subject. This inconsistency in tone toward the notion of artistic labor references the differing economies in which that labor circulates (see Figure 4).

This is further complicated by the strategic ambiguity of Okón's performance, which appears to be consciously speaking to the various registers of potential value against which the outward projection of the artistic persona might be measured. In one sense, the role of artist in *245 (d) 1* appears as a performance by Okón – every bit as staged as the actors he directs in *Shoot*. In his articulate explanatory statements, one can detect the refinement and savvy of a self-fashioned persona created for the realities of an art market increasingly dependent upon that persona as part of the commodity value of its work. In another sense, Okón's own performance cannot simplistically be written off as self-promotional; it also skillfully undermines *Inter-State*'s effort at putting documentary distance between it and the socio-economic milieu of the art world. Through performative hyperbole and artifice, Okón ironizes the convention of an authenticating 'artist statement,' and by so doing, disables *245 (d) 1*'s irreproachability. The documentary can no longer stand apart from the function of artistic labor, but becomes entrenched within it, co-implicated through their conjoined efforts toward publicity. In a contemporary art world invested in a star system that is almost indistinguishable from the entertainment industry, *Inter-State* can gain no meaningful traction against it, and it becomes clear that the documentary has, in effect, opened a publicity channel through which the accumulation of artistic cultural capital can be fed back into that system, helping to increase the mystique, exposure, circulation, and monetary value of both pieces. Perhaps the most salient aperçu of this overlap of interests is revealed by the fact that

Figure 4. Auditions in the Home Depot parking lot. *Inter-state: Video on the Go.* 2004. Courtesy LA Freewaves, Los Angeles.

it is the camera crew of *Inter-State* that shoots Okón's *Shoot*. The two works are not just intermarried symbolically but also materially and economically; like the fictive and factual interplay of the North Hollywood Shootout, *Shoot* and *Inter-State* are both doubly articulated – once as art, a second time as commerce. Devis and Okón appear like business partners in a mutually beneficial relationship that moves through interrelated sectors of the biopolitical economy; each plays an essential role in the production of the other's work. The two economies work in tandem, and the two artists speak from the access afforded to them through their cultural capital and their class privilege, which helps widen the circuit of and exchange and increase the value of their respective projects (see Figures 5 and 6).

Thus the project perpetually approaches the functional axis of labor by producing within itself a complex kind of auto-referential economy that not only mirrors and parallels but also directly connects to other economies adjacent to it. In the sinuous, indeterminate space between *Shoot* and *245 (d) 1*, something about the labor of art production is forcefully and unremittingly called into question – something that would rapidly retreat from view if either piece were taken only on its own terms. Their collaboration indicates the manner by which monetary and cultural value are produced in tandem and operate in rather similar and interpenetrating ways. From this view, the very questionable category 'art' can only be understood as something issued from a very nuanced integration of cultural capital and asset capital. Or to put it another way, for the artist and his or her work, the specific accumulation of asset capital is totally coextensive with, perhaps even subordinate to, the super-fluid circulation of cultural capital among segments of the art economy; consequently, the market value of art of is completely detached from a

Figure 5.   Devis (left) and Okón (right) direct actors at The Project. *Inter-state: Video on the Go*. 2004. Courtesy LA Freewaves, Los Angeles.

Figure 6. *Inter-state: Video on the Go.* 2004. Courtesy LA Freewaves, Los Angeles.

labor theory of value. The super-fluidity of Devis and Okón's own labor stands in stark contrast to other forms of undervalued labor necessary to their respective projects; their exchange obviates the mechanisms of cultural, class, and institutional privilege that enable artistic labor in becoming a speculative sign, capitalized far beyond the capacity of its material production. What is most fascinating about the Okón/Devis exchange is that despite this complicity with speculative value through an exchange that is available only to them, it seems that their co-production, intentionally or inadvertently, opens up spaces of new potentiality for the less fluid (and more exploitable) forms of labor that stand behind their co-production.

The post-industrial economy has occasioned a significant epistemological turn in the character of labor that recasts the very nature of what labor is, how it produces, how it is valued, how it enters subjectivity, and what it means and signifies. This way of understanding labor connects the juridical, political, and economic conditions of globalization to what Antonio Negri and Michael Hardt argue is a paradigm of biopolitical production, a purely productive form of power not based on the disciplinary repression of the subject, but rather on various forms of somatic production that are dispersed throughout, and immanent to the social body. All the spheres of art and culture, communication, welfare and care of the self, sexuality, language, information management, gender, the family, etc. are sites where biopolitics operates as a flexible form of internalized power that is more mercurial and adaptive than a disciplinary regime that maintains controls by means of coercion from within an institutional enclosure, such as a factory, a prison, or a school (Deleuze, 1992).

Without reproducing the complexities of their argument (a composite fusion of Foucault, Deleuze and Guattari, and new trends in Italian Marxism), I simply want to emphasize how they view biopolitical production as an essential way of accounting for two related aspects of immaterial labor: its modes of operation and a revised principle of exchange value extracted from that labor. In short, Hardt and Negri posit three primary modes of immaterial labor that are essential to the smooth functioning of the new global economic regime detailed above: communicative labor, interactive/symbolic labor, and affective labor. Their analysis attempts to rectify the tendency in the theories of immaterial labor singularly focused on its categorical lack of a material product. Their position shifts the emphasis from immateriality into the biopolitical context, that is, how labor itself performs the body and how it produces and reproduces itself. A second aspect related to immaterial labor is the way in which biopolitical production extends the superfluidity of monetary exchange into every element of social life. It is no longer enough to say that money has conquered the social sphere because it has become the measure of all things, but rather that money has conquered the social sphere because it has become indistinguishable from that sphere; money and the social body have become conjoined into a single undifferentiated field. Resonant of the Deleuzian desiring machine, biopolitical production has fully permeated the notion of value.

> From here we can see a horizon of values and a machine of distribution, a mechanism of accumulation and a means of circulation, a power and a language. There is nothing, no 'naked life,' no external standpoint, that can be posed outside this field permeated by money; nothing escapes money ... The great industrial and financial powers thus produce not only commodities but also subjectivities. They produce agentic subjectivities with the biopolitical context: they produce needs, social relations, bodies, and minds – which is to say, they produce producers. (Hardt & Negri, 2000, p. 32)

Day-laboring is often thought to epitomize a labor theory of value, in that the work of the laboring body has a direct correspondence to the mark of value in the form of wages. By all surface appearances, it seems to have a kind of self-evident quality about it: a laborer works for a fixed wage paid by the hour, job, or day, which are all in essence a correlative representation of the amount of productive force exerted by the laboring subject required to produce the commodity. But the misapplication of this common sense, neo-classical, Ricardian notion to a post-industrial global economy denies access of day-laboring to other productive circuits of value. Okón's *Shoot* invites a potential transvaluation of the delimitations of the labor theory of value by placing it into a new form of value based on biopolitical production, such as communicative labor or affective labor, the value of which has more fluidity in the global economy. Although Okón pays the laborers a fixed hourly rate, the laborers' task also becomes a site of affective, performative agency that expresses other forms of value that exceed that of the wage. Re-evaluating their activity according to communicative or affective measures of value opens that labor to entirely new circuits of exchange. The day-laborer hired as actor might potentially activate the same faculty used by the laborer in, say, a protest rally or another tactical disruption of established power.

Although the potential for this kind of agency is real, I want to also caution that such a claim is also contentious and problematic, nowhere more evident than in the divergent approaches by Devis and Okón toward the reference to the day-laborers' wage. What is concealed from the installation version of Okón's *Shoot* is uncomfortably reintroduced back into the economic circuit in the final sequence of *245 (d) 1*. Here the video takes a step back from its own complicity and polemically concludes by raising pointed ethical questions about exploitation that deliberately implicates the art world within an economic and cultural system that depends upon a vulnerable undervalued workforce in order to function (Neilson & Rossiter, 2005; Tari & Vanni, 2005). The sequence begins with a final voice-over narration of Okón making an artist's statement about the relationship of art and morality that accompanies a wide-angle, time-lapse dissolve of a trendy crowd inspecting the demolished police car at the opening of *Shoot*. In-between Okón's statements, Devis interjects several white on black intertitles that refer to the raw statistics and the economic conditions that are foundationally invisible to the chattering milieu of the art world sipping wine and networking at an opening where the travail of the labor that produced the piece has been effaced.

Intertitle: An estimated 8 to 12 million immigrants live in the US illegally
YO: I don't like representation or art that's moralistic in the sense that it has a very specific moral agenda.
Intertitle: The unauthorized labor force in the US totals 5.3 million workers
YO: Morality is a very complex issue and morality keeps changing over time, so I'm not interested in slogans and I'm not interested in telling people how they should behave.
Intertitle: Yoshua paid his workers $15 an hour for an 8 hour day
YO: I'm more interested in touching on aspects that move me and really interest me and that, most of the time, aspects that disturb me ... of the world ...
Intertitle: $120 for a day of work
YO: ... in order to collectively be able to consider them and put them on the table because many times a lot of these issues are just being ignored.
Intertitle: Shoot: 245 (d) 1

Labor theorist Hernando de Soto argues that it is not the accumulation of wealth, but rather the manipulation of property rights, titles, deeds contracts, and copyrights, that cumulatively produces the effect of capital. It is these formally adjudicated systems of enumeration and inscription that provide the social contract that enables the use of assets by providing them with potentiality, mobility, and currency. De Soto argues that if one were to enumerate the informal property assets of the world's poor, you would have a global wealth that exceeds the world's rich and multinational corporations many times over. Although his solution to this problem is ultimately places faith in the free market, the diagnosis is no less instructive: he argues that because these economies are informal and subterranean, and as a consequence immeasurable, they therefore lack fluidity and transferability and become what de Soto names 'dead capital' – capital that exists, yet cannot be leveraged. In a related argument Joseph Childers and Stephen Cullenberg refer to 'unremarked labor' as that labor that stands behind and supplements yet is elided from the value of official wage labor, such as women's domestic labor, 'third world' labor, children's labor, etc. If one were to transpose the arguments of de Soto and Childers and Cullenberg into the register of the media image, we might begin to rethink the potential recuperation of dead capital not just as a problem political economy but also one of culture.

By referencing the raw economic transaction between Okón and his actors, Devis introduces back into the circuit of exchange the 'dead capital' or 'unremarked labor' that is effaced from the piece itself – labor that is absolutely foundational to the operations of the upper strata of the economic hierarchy yet summarily excluded from circulating within that strata, the idea of which is equally applicable to the realm of cultural capital as it is to asset capital. It is exactly this reinscription of the unremarked that Devis introduces into what is otherwise effaced from *Shoot*. In a cadence of ironic counterpoint, Okón's remarks about raising pertinent social issues within a framework of moral relativism is directly contested by Devis' own reinscription of what is excluded from *Shoot*: the wages paid to the actors for their labor, the surplus value extracted from that labor through a complex system of publicity and exchange, and the unspoken collusion of the gallery system and the entertainment industry. Paradoxically, by completely insinuating itself into the production of Okón's *Shoot* and becoming complicit with the economic strata that benefits from the exploitation of the surplus labor of others, *245 (d) 1* is finally able to produce an oblique critique of its own project along the functional axis by pointing to the shared labor necessary to the co-production, a critique that subtly undermines the commercial format of the piece.

On the other hand, the moral emphasis on the financial transaction between *Okón* and his actors at the conclusion of *Inter-State* might be precisely the kind of critique that reverts the video's labor politics to the representational axis by playing into a romantic cliché of the sweat and toil of the poor, a cliché that *Shoot* is careful to avoid. From the auditions outside the Home Depot and the footage in Okón's installation, it seems evident that while at the same time *Shoot* is exploitative of its participants monetarily, it also opens a space (as do all forms of labor) for the improvised creativity of the worker to exceed the constraints of the system. But much of the improvisation, too, must undoubtedly come from each actor's deeply personal relationship to being an undocumented worker in the US, likely crossing the border to escape one form of the abuse of state power only to confront another. Here *Okón*'s moral relativism might be essential in clearing a space for the actors to perform their fantasies about the demise of repressive state power – allegorized by the death of the police. Yet this emerges not, as Okón intimates, out of the construction of a kind of open or free space, but precisely because it is not free – precisely because the framework he sets up is itself part of a interwoven complex of social and economic power that no amount of critical distance and self-reflexive irony can overcome. In the final codicil of the film, Devis tempers this optimism by suggesting to the actors that perhaps he and Okón were collaborators in the scene of a crime. In an exit interview with one of the actors, Onoris Montiel, he interrogates her about her experience on the set of *Shoot* with her back up against the white wall of the gallery as if in a police line up (see Figure 7).

> JD: Did you find it Strange that Yoshua hired you without having any acting
> experience?
> OM: No, because this … is the country of opportunities and if he doesn't
> give us the chance, well he wouldn't have any actors.

With ambiguous optimism, Montiel draws upon a rehearsed but ironic platitude of the American dream as a way of producing her own power and agency over the scene. There is something in her statement – and her performance – that eludes both exploitation and social critique, the moral ambiguity of Okón and the sober realism of Devis, the artist and social documentarian, and points to an altogether different space of value that evades the sights of both gunmen, a value that is unremarked, self-defined, and invisible to the circuits of exchange, but is no less real.

Figure 7.   Onoris Montiel is interviewed about the experience of acting in *Shoot. Inter-state: Video on the Go.* 2004. Courtesy LA Freewaves, Los Angeles.

Note

1. Although purportedly I am referring to two independent works here, I maintain that there is a level of intextricability that requires the Devis/Okón collaboration be interpreted as single project.

References

Childers, J., & Cullenberg, S. (2000). *Speculating with value/gambling with difference: Spivak's Marx*. Retrieved 20 February 2005 from http://www.economics.ucr.edu/papers/papers00/index.html.

De Soto, H. (2000). *The mystery of capital: Why capitalism triumphs in the west and fails everywhere else.* New York: Basic Books.

Debroise, O. (Ed.). (2006). *La era de la discrepancia: Arte y cultura visual en México 1968–1997* [The age of discrepanies: Art and visual culture in México 1968–97]. México DF: Turner Publications and Universidad Nacional Autónoma de México.

Deleuze, G. (1992). Postscript on the societies of control. *October, 59,* 3–7.

Dorfsman, A., & Okon, Y. (Eds.). (2005). *La panadería, 1994–2002.* México DF: Editorial Turner de México.

Foley, S. (1981). *Space time sound: Conceptual art in the San Francisco Bay area: The 70s.* Seattle: University of Washington Press.

Fusco, C. (2001). The unbearable weightness of beings: Art in Mexico after NAFTA. In *The bodies that were not ours: And other writings* (pp. 61–77). New York: Routledge.

Hardt, M., & Negri, A. (2000). *Empire.* Cambridge: Harvard University Press.

Hardt, M., & Negri, A. (2004). *Multitude: War and democracy in the age of empire.* New York: Penguin.

Harvey, D. (2005). *A brief history of neoliberalism.* New York: Oxford University Press.

Krauss, R. (1990). The cultural logic of the late capitalist museum. *October, 54,* 3–17.

Marx, K. (1973). *Grundrisse.* New York: Penguin.

Neilson, B., & Rossiter, N. (2005). From precarity to precariousness and back again: Labour, life and unstable networks. *Fibre Culture,* 5. Retrieved 10 January 2007 from http://journal.fibreculture.org/issue5/.

O'Dell, K. (2000). Time clocks and paradox: On labor and temporality in performance art. In J. Schall (Ed.), *Tempus fugit: Time flies* (pp. 158–171). Seattle: University of Washington Press.

Okón, Y. (n.d.). Retrieved 11 November 2006 from http://www.yoshuaokon.com.

Ramírez, M.C. (1999). Tactics for thriving on adversity: Conceptualism in Latin America, 1960–1980. In L. Camnitzer, J. Farver, & R. Weiss (Eds.), *Global conceptualism: Points of origin 1950s–1980s* (pp. 53–71). New York: Queens Museum of Art.

Riis, J. (1890). *How the other half lives: Studies among the tenements of New York*. New York: Charles Scribner's Sons.

Rorimer, A. (2001). *New art in the 60s and 70s: Redefining reality*. London: Thames and Hudson.

Sekula, A. (1978). Dismantling modernism, reinventing documentary (notes on the Politics of Representation). *Massachusetts Review*, Summer, 859–883.

Sekula, A. (1992). The body and the archive. In R. Bolton (Ed.), *The contest of meaning: Critical histories of photography* (pp. 343–389). Cambridge: MIT Press.

Tagg, J. (1993). *The burden of representation: Essays on photographies and histories*. Minneapolis: University of Minnesota Press.

Tari, M., & Vanni, I. (2005). On the life and deeds of San Precario, patron saint of precarious workers and lives. *Fibre Culture,* 5. Retrieved 10 January 2007 from http://journal.fibreculture.org/issue5/

Wall, J. (1995). Marks of indifference: Aspects of photography in, or as, conceptual art. In A. Goldstein & A. Rorimer (Eds.), *Reconsidering the object of art: 1965–1975* (pp. 246–267). Cambridge: MIT Press.

What time is this picture? Cameraphones, tourism, and the digital gaze in Japan

M.D. Foster

Department of Folklore and Ethnomusicology and the Department of East Asian Languages and Cultures, Indiana University

After its introduction in 2000, the cameraphone (a cell phone with digital camera functionality) rapidly became a ubiquitous presence in Japan, part of an increase in non-voice modalities associated with mobile telephony. This essay employs an experimental format to explore what it means to combine cell phone and camera in a single portable device. Particular attention is paid to how cameraphones, within the broader context of cell phone (*keitai*) culture in Japan, alter the way tourist sites and events are experienced, recorded, and shared. Ultimately, the ease with which the cameraphone facilitates capture, narrativization, sharing, and deletion of photos, causes a blurring of traditional distinctions between the touristic and the everyday. Furthermore, these changes are imbricated in a broader cultural shift in perception and consciousness engendered by the continued interplay between producers of digital technologies and creative use of these technologies by consumers.

Catching a fish

Summer, 2004. Enoshima Aquarium.

It is a sweltering, sweaty Saturday at this aquarium about an hour south of Tokyo. Outside, young couples in designer clothes, wrap-around sunglasses, and white sunhats stroll hand-in-hand. Groups of middle-school students flirt and laugh. Boisterous children yank at the bothered, tired hands of their parents. Inside, it is dark and hot and packed with visitors. Around each smooth, glowing tank, a crowd pushes in to glimpse whatever colorful sea creature is cruising silently inside. Small children worm their way up to the front and press their faces against the cold glass, staring open-mouthed. But for most of us, the jeweled fish inside are completely obscured by the humans hankering to see them. All we can do is read the label above the tank – hammerhead shark, clown fish, electric eel – and imagine what the thing looks like.

That's when I first notice it. A young man at the back of the crowd releases his girlfriend's hand. He flicks open a slick red cell phone and lifts it up above the heads of the spectators in front of him, angled down toward the tank and the invisible fish inside. He holds the phone still for an instant, clicks the shutter, and then brings it back down again. He cradles it in his hand like a treasure as he and his girlfriend peer down at the screen. They smile at each other, and move on to the next tank.

Suddenly I realize that many people are doing this. This digitally facilitated periscopic vision is apparently a new-fangled way of seeing the sights. Already removed from their natural environment, these fish are doubly decontextualized now, appearing tiny and still and silent on the viewing screen of a cameraphone. People who have paid the full price of admission will take away with them dozens of photos of their experience, but possibly never 'see' a single fish.

Perception/speed

My experience at the aquarium set me on contemplating the importance of the combination of mobile phone and camera. It seemed clear even in 2004 that the invention and rapid proliferation of phones equipped with cameras was subtly shifting the way events both mundane and extraordinary were experienced. This was especially true in Japan, where cell phones had very rapidly become omnipresent. And it seemed to me also that tourism – in all its many forms – might provide a metonymically instructive example of this change in perception.

As I began actively observing the use of cameraphones over the next few years, I soon realized that however perceptive my ruminations may have been in 2004, they were now already out of date. But this, of course, is part of a much larger issue that informs any discourse and practice based on new technologies: the question of *speed*, by which I mean the immediacy of image capture, evaluation, and transfer, and also the velocity by which technology itself – and our acceptance of it – changes. In 1965 Intel co-founder Gordon E. Moore famously observed that the number of transistors on an integrated circuit would (continue to) double approximately every two years (Moore, 1965). 'Moore's Law', as the observation came to be called, has proven prescient or at least remarkably powerful as a self-fulfilling prophecy. Strictly speaking, the law originally refers to transistor size and production cost, but it has also come to articulate the dizzying pace of technological innovation and market growth. Ultimately the law also reflects consumer reception – bewildered, enthralled, accepting – of new technologies. Any technological innovation is nothing more than a passing phase: movement may be exponential, but it is non-teleological, premised on the notion that the technology you are holding in your hand is only a single step in a process with no end. By considering one small ripple in this rapid flux – the cameraphone in Japan – we also glimpse how change and speed, and the speed of change, become integrated into the circuits of everyday life.

Emergent

The development of cell phone technology and its commercial implementation varies from country to country, contingent on combinations of cultural, legal, political, and economic factors (Katz & Aakhus, 2002; Agar, 2003; Ito, 2005). The camera function is part of a trend in non-voice modalities, such as internet access and text messaging, that in Japan have surpassed voice communication in popularity (Okabe & Ito, 2006, p. 80; also Matsuda, 2005; Okada, 2005). (The phenomenal success of the iPhone reflects this global trend toward multi-media mobile devices.) Because of the heterogeneity of users – in terms of socio-economic factors, nationality, gender, age, education, etc. – multifaceted research into cameraphone usage often demands innovative ethnographic and empirical methodologies (see e.g., Okabe & Ito, 2006; Ito, Okabe, & Anderson, forthcoming; Van House & Davis, 2005). The project is made all the more intricate, and all the more interesting, by the fact that cameraphone usages are emergent practices driven by rapid technological innovation combined with consumer creativity. What pictures are taken, why they are taken, who they are taken by, how they are used – all of this is part of a complex dance between technology producers and consumers.[1]

Scholars who have researched cameraphones in the US divide usage patterns into three broad classifications: memory-capture, communication, and expression. More specifically, cameraphones facilitate processes of memory creation/preservation (both group and personal), maintenance of social relations, self-presentation and self-expression (Van House & Davis, 2005). In Japan, where cameraphones became widespread relatively early, broad categories of usage are generally similar. Okabe & Ito (2006), for example, classify emergent practices as 'personal archiving', 'intimate visual co-presence' (i.e., sharing of photos), and 'peer-to-peer news and reporting'. While my own comments here implicitly support these analyses, I am less interested in categorizing the ways cameraphones are used than in trying to apprehend how an emergent technology both fits into and alters existing cultural practices. In particular, I set out not to observe everyday life per se, but rather the use of the cameraphone in (domestic) tourism, when the user temporarily (and voluntarily) enters a situation distinct from the quotidian, a place/event that is somehow different and therefore, perhaps, picture-worthy.

My discussion is based on yearly fieldwork in Japan (since 2000), primarily in the summer months, during which I have joined visitors at a range of tourist sites and events throughout the archipelago, including shrines, temples, local festivals, museums, aquariums, zoos, historic buildings, and street performances; I have also spoken with numerous cameraphone users. Despite, or because of, this varied immersion, I hesitate to offer a sweeping theoretical conclusion, but present piecemeal thoughts on the way digital media forges a contemporary tourist gaze that adapts to existing structures even as it indelibly alters them. Through the course of my observations I gradually came to realize that one critical way cameraphones do affect tourist practices is, in fact, by subverting the very premise of my own investigations – that is, *by making the distinction between tourism and everyday life increasingly irrelevant*. In the scenes that follow, traditional notions of tourism ultimately serve only as a touchstone whose shape becomes more and more hazy with the cameraphone's growing presence in people's lives.

Oxymoronics

The cameraphone is oxymoronic, linking two seemingly incongruent elements to create an original whole. Strictly speaking, as Michel de Certeau notes, the elements of an oxymoron 'are not true opposites'. Camera and phone do not cancel each other out. The uses made possible by their amalgamation do not suggest 'unsurmountable tension' but rather 'the value of fullness' (de Certeau, 1992, p. 143): they embody a hybrid (or perhaps a whole new species) that simultaneously redefines each component of its making.[2] Furthermore, the cameraphone is part of an integrating – or at least a readjustment – of a whole series of other ostensibly incongruous pairs: permanence/ephemerality, time/space, original/replica, tourist/site, here/there.

Cameraphones, it has been observed, occupy 'a dynamic niche in a rapidly changing scene of digital photography, image circulation, and visual culture' and therefore 'theories of the aesthetics and cultural dynamics of cell phone photography are rather precarious at this historical moment' (Goggin, 2006, p. 153). With this in mind, in the few pages that follow I present a sequence of precarious ruminations about cameraphones and tourism not to prognosticate on media and modalities for the future, nor to theorize a 'new type of photography' (Kato, Okabe, Ito & Uemoto, 2005, p. 307), but simply to archive – as one might with a cameraphone – small scenes of change within the maelstrom of this particularly volatile historical moment. This format reflects the technology itself: a series of pictures scrolled across a single screen, some images more detailed than others, some directly connected, some overlapping and redundant, others leaping in time and place, but all contributing to a temporary and mutable completeness that can readily be expanded or have parts deleted, and ultimately loops back to the very first picture, now somehow differently interpretable. Take away or add a picture or two and the story is still complete, though the narrative is different.

Whether successful or not, at the very least this experimental approach reflects the fractured and changing ways in which cameraphones have started to infiltrate contemporary consciousnesses. As an emergent and unsettled mode of communication/perception/archiving, the cameraphone demands, I think, fresh academic methodologies and novel ways of cultural critique. It is also significant that the precarious observations generated by such an experimental approach will soon themselves become historical relics – snapshots of last year's vacation – as technologies and their uses continue to proliferate in unforeseeable directions.

Generation gap(s)

On the occasion of the birth of his daughter in 1997, French–born American inventor and entrepreneur Philippe Kahn sent photographs through a cell phone jerry–rigged to a digital camera. Whether or not this actually constitutes the first cameraphone is open to debate, and depends ultimately on how you choose to define cameraphone (Kanellos, 2007), but it is clear that the first commercially produced cameraphones were introduced in Japan in 2000 (and North America two years later). The product took off when J–Phone (now SoftBank Mobile) marketed a handset with a camera to coincide with a service called *sha-meru* or 'photo-email'. DoCoMo and AU soon followed (with 'i-shot' and 'photo-mail' respectively); by March 2003 some 29.3 percent of cell phone service subscribers already had cameraphones, a total of 22.21 million people (Okada, 2005, p. 56). While cameraphones were initially most popular among users in their teens and twenties (Okada, 2005, p. 56), the growth of their market share has been explosive (see also Ishino 2008, pp. 41–45). By 2005 'almost all' mobile phones sold in Japan were cameraphones (Steinbock, 2005, p. 185).

An early Japanese television commercial features a grizzled old man taking a picture of his family. He lines them up, tells them to say cheese, and holds up his telephone to snap the shot. The family laughs at him, and one of them shouts,

'Grandpa, that's not a camera, that's a phone!' The old man smiles knowingly, comments quietly on how behind the times they are, and takes the shot.

'Weapons of mass photography'[3]

'With this kind of device', Philippe Kahn predicted, 'you're going to see the best and the worst of things' (quoted in Parks, 2000, p. 3). By 2004, the cameraphone had already made its mark on the global political and emotional landscape: such devices were used to take and transmit many of the pictures of torture at the Abu Ghraib prison. Soon afterwards, rumors circulated about a ban on wireless consumer technology within the US military. Though no such ban occurred, Donald Rumsfeld's comments on 7 May 2004 betray a paranoia of the potential of this new technology: 'People', Rumsfeld whined, 'are running around with digital cameras and taking these unbelievable photographs and passing them off, against the law, to the media, to our surprise, when they had not even arrived in the Pentagon' (quoted in Jardin, 2004; see also Goggin, 2006, p. 147). The ability to take a picture at any time and any place and immediately transmit it somewhere else creates a multi-optic web of surveillance, a cynical twist on the traditional panoptic society. As anthropologist Mizuko Ito has noted,

> The cat's already out of the bag, but what's striking about what we're seeing now is that it's very unlike the top-down, Big Brother surveillance we normally associate with the idea of other people watching you. This is a bottom-up, 'little brother', peer-to-peer type of surveillance. (quoted in Jardin, 2004)

That is, cameraphones – whether resistant or complicit with dominant ideological structures – represent the potential for a kind of decentralized, rhizomatic form of surveillance and communication.[4]

An age of wondrous machines

For better or for worse, it is clear that handheld technology has given humans, especially in economically privileged regions, what would have until recently been considered superhuman powers. While driving through London on a Saturday morning, one of novelist Ian McEwan's characters opines,

> ... if the present dispensation is wiped out now, the future will look back on us as gods ... lucky gods blessed by supermarket cornucopias, torrents of accessible information, warm clothes that weigh nothing, extended lifespans, wondrous machines. This is an age of wondrous machines. Portable telephones barely bigger than your ear. Whole music libraries held in an object the size of a child's hand. Cameras that can beam their snapshots around the world. (McEwan, 2005, p. 77)

London calling

The 7 July 2005 bombings in the London underground were the first time in history cameraphones were used to document news on a major scale. The *Washington Post* reported:

> One blurry, poorly lighted image was captured yesterday by the phone of a subway passenger trapped underground along with dozens of others following the series of

lethal explosions that crippled London during its morning commute. The door of the subway car, stopped in a tunnel at King's Cross, is pried open to give passengers air, which hangs thick with smoke. Within hours, the image made its way onto television screens and Web sites, prompting one online respondent to post the message 'watching this on the news in the U.S., praying for you all'. (Noguchi, 2005)

The lag-time of transmission and the filters of institutional journalism are all but absent here; subject and object collide in a frenzied instance of time-space compression; there is no breathing room. News is (virtually) immediate and (virtually) everywhere, inspiring (virtual) empathy across continents.

The extreme context of the London bombings highlights a critical dual function of the mobile phone itself, as both an intimate, personal mode of communication and one with devastatingly public ramifications. 'When faced with a catastrophe', scholars note,

> it is the small hand-held device in our pockets we turn to, both to re-connect ourselves with our loved-ones in the outside world and also to capture the events we are part of. It expresses a double interpretation of our presence in the world – both '*I* am here' and 'I am *here*'. (Glotz, Bertschi & Locke, 2005, p. 12)

Accidental journalism

The subversive potential of 'citizen journalism' is evident, for example, in the cameraphone video that captured the hanging of Saddam Hussein. The shaky grainy footage not only makes us witnesses to the hanging but also to its illicit recording – for which arrests were made. As in the medium-is-the-message formula, technology not only covers the news, it *makes* the news. The immediacy of transmission guarantees that even if the photographer is seized on the spot, the images may have already been released to the world.

Needless to say, however, cameraphone journalism is being co-opted by institutionalized media: less then two weeks after the London bombings, the *New York Times* reported that a local television affiliate had 'started soliciting cellphone pictures and amateur video . . . from people who witness a news event'. The article went on to quote NBC news executive Mark Lukasiewicz: 'Now millions of people have the ability not only to tell you what they are seeing, but to show it . . . It is transformational technology' (Cohen, 2005).

Keitai culture

In Japan, the cell phone is called a *keitai denwa*, which can be translated roughly as 'carry-able' (*keitai*) 'telephone' (*denwa*). Since at least 1995, the device has commonly been referred to simply as a *keitai* (Matsuda, 2005, p. 20; Fujikawa, 2008, pp. 12–14), which Kohiyama Kenji suggests is on the way to becoming a globally recognized term similar to 'sushi' (Kohiyama, 2005, pp. 3–4). This abbreviation, which distinctly elides the word *denwa*, is all the more appropriate now that the panoply of non-voice functions – from internet functionality to built-in calculator – far outnumber traditional telephonic uses (Kohiyama, 2005; Matsuda, 2005). To carry your keitai means to be armed with an entire kit of functions personalizable and adaptable to your everyday life; the keitai is, as Ito puts it, 'not so much about a new technical capability of freedom of motion, but about a snug and intimate technosocial tethering' (Ito, 2005, p. 1). Within this context, perhaps it is not surprising that by 2007 the keitai had even given birth to an entirely new literary genre, the so-called *keitai shôsetsu* or keitai-novel, short fictional texts written on, and readable on, the screen of a keitai (see Ishino, 2008, pp. 45–51). *Keitai* indexes more than just a mobile phone or even a piece of equipment: it is a *mentalité*, a culture.

The ubiquity of this keitai culture in Japan cannot be overemphasized. For many young people in particular, life without a keitai is all but unimaginable (Kato, 2005). A recent film, a romantic comedy entitled *Babaru e go!! Taimu mashin wa doramu shiki* (Kameyama, 2007; English title: Bubble fiction: Boom or bust), features a protagonist who travels seventeen years back in time to a pre-keitai Tokyo of 1990. While articulating a nostalgia for small differences in fashion and musical styles, the film also thematizes the way in which the advent of the keitai has indelibly changed social interactions. To the young protagonist, the keitai is a prosthetic device enabling her to function in everyday life; she is at a loss without it, unable even to arrange a meeting at the train station. In the film, the actual 'time machine' is, comically, a laundry machine. But the repeated references to the keitai suggest that it might be interpreted similarly, as a commonplace mechanism through which people (voices and images) are transported from one place to another, making otherwise unimaginable communication possible.

Tribe of the thumb

The generation of keitai savvy users has been dubbed the *oyayubi-zoku*, literally 'thumb-tribe' or 'thumb-family' because of its facility with rapid input using only the thumbs, a facility that, according to some observers, may also transfigure practices such as pointing and ringing doorbells (Plant, 2001, p. 53). Notably, this agility of the thumb seems to have started in Japan around the year 2000 and then appeared elsewhere around the world (Glotz, Bertschi & Locke, 2005, pp. 12–13). The designation as a separate 'tribe' or 'family' not only gestures to the generational gap between keitai-facile users and those still awkwardly inputting numbers with their index fingers, but also suggests a new branch of an evolutionary tree, in which the opposable human thumb facilitates new modalities of communication.

Killing dead time

The conversion of otherwise 'wasted' hours into productive labor was at the heart of the introduction of mobile telephony. The ability to communicate anywhere at anytime was vaunted in Britain, for example, in a 1985 advertisement urging consumers to turn their 'dead time' into 'genuine productive hours' (quoted in Agar, 2003, p. 83). To be sure, on the streets of Tokyo today, one still overhears business conversations conducted via cell phone. But the keitai (and so-called *poke-beru* pagers before them) inspired a broad based telecommunications revolution through the 1990s that quickly transcended the limited industrial/financial framework for which they were originally conceived (Fujimoto, 2005). In contemporary Japan, the keitai has saturated almost all socio-economic strata to become a common part of growing up Japanese, carried by younger and younger school children (Miyaki, 2005) and used for all manner of social and recreational purposes. The addition of camera functionality only reinforces the varied non-productive, social applications of the device.

More to the point, like the keitai in general, the cameraphone embodies a dialectic between 'serious' and 'playful' practices, creating a continuum between the recreational and the instrumental. A salaryman in his late thirties told me that he uses the camera function to snap photos of bus and train timetables when traveling for both business and pleasure. This saves him the bother of noting down the schedule for his return journey, and he can just delete the photo when his trip is over. A schoolteacher in her late thirties explained that she often uses her cameraphone when shopping alone for clothes. She can snap a picture of an item she is considering purchasing and send it to a friend for an immediate second opinion. The cameraphone operates in the 'service of capital' (Agar, 2003, p. 83) here, but simultaneously creates a sense of 'intimate visual co-presence' (Okabe & Ito, 2006, p. 91), tapping into already existing social networks.

Mass transit

One reason, I would suggest, that keitai culture developed so rapidly in Japan is because of the pervasiveness of trains. In expansive conurbations and suburbs people commute to work, school, and play on an intricate network of convenient and usually punctual trains. Initially keitai use on trains was a controversial social issue (Okabe & Ito, 2005, pp. 205–218). Now, however, commuters have internalized the keitai etiquette of not disturbing fellow passengers and it is rare to hear a ringtone or a voice conversation. On the other hand, a remarkable number of passengers can be seen thumbing away at their keitai, checking the internet, texting, sending email, reviewing appointments, playing games, reading a keitai-novel, or scrolling through pictures. Even on overcrowded trains, where it is too packed to unfold a newspaper and difficult even to turn the pages of a paperback book, a keitai can be held close to the body; very little elbowroom is required to input with your thumbs. The spectacular success of keitai in Japan – particularly non-voice applications – stems from the ample 'dead time' specific to a culture with a well-used mass transit system.

Reframe

The 3 October 2005 cover of *The New Yorker* perceptively marked a reframing of visual discourses, illustrating that even the Empire State Building and all it symbolizes can be instantaneously re-encoded into an emblem you can hold in your hand (Figure 1). In the same year, a brochure for the Toyota Corolla also reflected the valuation created by the digital frame: on the cover, a 2005 Corolla is framed in a cameraphone viewfinder, an exquisite miniature no larger than the fingers grasping the phone (Toyota Motor Sales, 2004). A sight worth seeing, it seems, is also worth capturing and (perhaps) sharing. The cameraphone simultaneously allows for both of these operations. It is a friendly medium, aestheticizing, shrinking, and managing the world-out-there and the big and sometimes beautiful things in it.

The example of these two images – one a unique modernist landmark, the other representative of early twenty-first-century mass-production – brings home two seemingly contradictory powers of the cameraphone operating within the cultural imaginary. While the monumental Empire State Building is shrunk into the everyday

Figure 1.   Cover of *The New Yorker*, 3 October 2005.

frame of the cameraphone, inversely a mundane car (for 'Everyday People', as the late 1990s Toyota commercial explained) is elevated to the status of work of art. Is the 'aura' of the original destroyed when distance is erased and a great landmark is digitized and carried in the pocket like a fetish? Or does it become a personalized, handcrafted reproduction, all the more meaningful (and auratic) for its subtle uniqueness, for the slight shade of difference from one cameraphone to the next? And what of the Toyota Corolla: does this commonplace vehicle acquire a whole new meaning, an aura (a corolla?), when framed, miniaturized, and admired?

Digital tourism

In Japan, domestic tourism is big business; flocks of visitors young and old tour the nation in the summer, on weekends, on school holidays. Some of this movement is seasonal, as certain areas are known for the blossoming of their azaleas or plum trees or for the celebration of a particular festival, but often people will simply visit, dutifully, famous shrines, temples and historical places. Personal photographic documentation of these pilgrimages has been a part of Japanese tourist practice since the advent of the camera. Amateur photography is still an extraordinarily popular hobby, but now of course the cameraphone provides an easier, more immediate mode of authenticating one's visit. It encourages a facile and instantaneous transformation of the boundless tourist experience – haptic, tactile, olfactory – into a virtual event, a bounded (framed) visual text that can be played with as a game: manipulated, transferred, saved, sent, and ultimately, deleted. 'Around town, and particularly at tourist spots', Okabe and Ito (2006, p. 79) note, 'the sounds of the camera phone's shutter have become an unremarkable part of the setting'.

Authentication and aura

Through (often) an exchange of money, tourists achieve 'temporary rights of possession of places away from home', and with it temporary ownership of 'visual property' (Lash & Urry, 1994, p. 271). Photography extends those rights, allowing the viewer to extract and keep a piece of that visual property. Accordingly, photography structures tourism and tourism structures photography. As Crouch and Lübbren (2003, p. 8) note, 'the tourist participates in the provided gaze and, on cue, follows its lead in the structuring of space, culture, and spectacle'. There is almost an obligation to photograph certain sites and scenes. In this way a narrative is shaped and the public site, the must-see or the viewing spot, becomes one's own, part of a personal story that can be shared. Tied to this narrative is what John Urry calls a 'hermeneutic circle' in which the tourist feels obligated to snap a shot that replicates a famous image from a tourist brochure, TV, or website. Proof of the experience relies on the similarity of the captured images to those viewed in anticipation of the journey (Urry, 2002, p.129). These are non-unique pictures valuable explicitly for their similarity to so many others. Cameraphone photography spins this hermeneutic circle even tighter, inspiring not only a more pervasive distribution of images, but also enabling the tourist to communicate the veracity of the experience through a real time transfer from the 'field' to 'home'.

Perhaps with the cameraphone, it is not so much that authenticity (or desire for it) is now irrelevant, but that a handset-sized text that can be shared with others becomes in itself an expression of something authentic. Indeed, the fact that you can send an image from the *place* it is occurring at the *time* it is occurring intensifies its indexicality and imbues it with a sort of super-authenticity: it is a reproduction, to be sure, but it is an authentic reproduction. The receiver of the image can experience the same visual text through the almost identical frame of his or her own handheld screen at almost the same time. But while there may indeed be a sense of co-presence between sender and receiver, this sense is anything but pure. To coin another oxymoron, it is a distant proximity, for the very immediacy and presence of the image received also underscores the physical distance between receiver and sender, between the object in its ambient context and a disembodied two-dimensional sign on the cameraphone screen. And as Walter Benjamin tells us, a key factor of the aura is 'the unique phenomenon of a distance, however close it may be' (Benjamin, 1968, p. 222); the cameraphone can create, as it were, a unique phenomenon of closeness, however distant it may be.

Tourist-flâneur-photographer

The 'strolling *flâneur*' of the late nineteenth century, Urry (2002, p. 127) points out, was 'a forerunner of the twentieth-century tourist and in particular of the activity which has in a way become emblematic of the tourist: the democratised taking of photographs'. Susan Sontag (1977, p. 55) also makes this connection between the perambulating observer and the dream of photography: 'The photographer', she says,

> is an armed version of the solitary walker reconnoitering, stalking, cruising the urban inferno, the voyeuristic stroller who discovers the city as a landscape of voluptuous extremes. Adept of the joys of watching, connoisseur of empathy, the *flâneur* finds the world 'picturesque'.

One hundred years later, in the voluptuous extremes of the early twenty-first century, the ubiquity, at least in Japan, of cameraphones has further democratized Urry's 'taking of photographs'. The voyeur is no longer consciously armed with a camera, for the camera is inseparable from the phone, which itself has become a cyborgian appendage to the human of the era. A camera hanging around the neck or dangling from the hand is no longer the badge of the tourist – the cameraphone does not distinguish the walker in any overt way. And this walker may or may not be solitary: the very mechanism for communication with others is part of the gadget. No longer can we know, just by looking, whether somebody is alone.

Historicity machine

The cameraphone embodies an age of ephemerality. It captures the fleeting moment, lets you archive in miniature the instant as it was just an instant ago. Frederic Jameson (1991, p. 284) has described historicity as 'a perception of the present as history; that is, as a relationship to the present which somehow defamiliarizes it and allows us that distance from immediacy which is at length characterized by historical perspective'. A cameraphone does just this, freezing and framing and defamiliarizing the 'thing' or the 'event', providing an immediate and almost unmediated historical perspective. It is a machine that slows down time: users can scroll through recently captured images, reliving in slow motion, with ellipses and jumps like a flickering old-time movie, the experience they have just had. The relationship with time is paradoxical – even as time is slowed down and past moments linger on the cameraphone screen, the minutiae of change are highlighted, the images already remnants of something no longer (in the) present.

Instant nostalgia

A sunny June day at the Jôjuin, a Kamakura temple famous for its hydrangea. Crowds throng a long stone stairway meandering through an explosion of blossoms in pastel shades of blue and pink. At the top of the stairway, slightly off to the side, three twentysomething women gather in a circle, gazing down at a cameraphone. They shade the viewfinder from the sunlight and scroll through pictures of flowers and of themselves posing with the flowers, nostalgic for moments just past, for sites only a few feet away. This excited longing to hold onto (and share) the past, no matter how recent, makes sense within the logic of tourism and cameraphones. Now everything can be documented, archived, and kept: nothing has to be given up or given away. You can infinitely reproduce a single image, transmit it to dozens of other phones, and it never actually leaves your hand.

Object of the gaze

If the digital image captured at the site is a way of creating a souvenir, of making material the sentient, affective experience, then it is an immaterial materiality, as ephemeral as it is easily captured. As a tourist commodity, its value is akin to an utterance in conversation – no coincidence that the mode of exchange is a telephone. If the proliferation of photographs is no more than the production of ephemera, then the very evanescence of each image also alters its function. The act of 'snapping the shutter' removes the scene from the viewer (and the viewer from the scene) by immediately decontextualizing the experience: the tiny viewing screen of the cameraphone itself becomes the object of the tourist gaze. The unbounded space of the event is translated into material evidence, made real – even as it is being experienced – only by the framed digital image (Figure 2).

Figure 2. Penguins and visitors at the Asahikawa Zoo in Hokkaido.

Everyday and commonplace

Okabe and Ito have noted that, 'In comparison to the traditional camera, which gets trotted out for special excursions and events – noteworthy moments bracketed off from the mundane – camera phones capture the more fleeting and unexpected moments of surprise, beauty and adoration in the everyday' (Okabe & Ito, 2003). The camera allows the user to make remarkable that which may have gone unnoticed before; through apprehending and freezing a thing or event digitally, 'the mundane is elevated to a photographic object' (Okabe & Ito, 2003). The keitai itself becomes a repository, a personal archive of one's most recent experiences, a museum curated by the self. The cameraphone is a quotidian device, carried in the pocket along with keys and wallet, that 'makes photography "commonplace", stripping it of every intention other than for one's immediate pleasure and the pleasure of expressing something in the immediate present' (Rivière, 2005, p. 171). In one sense, perhaps, the constant presence of a machine for documenting everyday events encourages visual acuity and an increased sensitivity for small shades of difference and 'serendipitous sightings' (Kato et al., 2005, p. 305). Cameraphone users seek the thing that stands out just a little bit, the anomaly that pricks their interest, the *punctum* as Roland Barthes (1981) might call it, that is (or is *made*) meaningful within the miniature frame of the cameraphone screen.

Of scenery and people

In a 2006 survey of 300 people between the ages of 18 and 50, some 234 indicated that they use the camera function of their keitai for more than one picture per month (99.6 percent take 'still' photos). When asked what they photographed, 73.8 percent selected 'scenery and landscapes' (*fûkei / keshiki*), followed by 'people' (*jinbutsu*) at 71.7 percent. 77.6 percent of survey respondents felt the camera function to be a 'necessary' (*hitsuyô*) component of their keitai, leading the surveyors to conclude simply that, 'As they develop, keitai cameras seem to be becoming a necessary part of people's lifestyles' (japan.internet.com, 2006). More recent statistics confirm this trend: in 2008, some 36.3% (the highest single response) of respondents indicated that the camera was 'the function most important in choosing which type of cell phone to purchase' (Ishino, 2008, pp. 42–43).

Tourism and counter-tourism

As a technological appendage, the keitai allows moments throughout the day to be captured casually in visual form. In contrast to such everyday experience, however, tourism is an active practice whereby one chooses to seek something out of the ordinary and prepares for the experience by, for example, taking along a camera. The advent of the cameraphone-as-appendage allows the casual tourist to leave this 'extra' camera behind, something many people have been doing – since 2003, cameraphones have outsold digital cameras worldwide (Van House, Davis, Takhteyev, Ames, & Finn, 2004, p. 2). But what does it mean to use an everyday device to capture not-so-everyday sites and events? The keitai facilitates a double operation here: it has the power to transform the mundane into something unusual, framing and defamiliarizing otherwise overlooked fragments of daily life; and it can also – through a similar dynamic of (re)framing – make something out of the ordinary seem familiar. That is to say, cameraphones encourage an easy play between the everyday and the extraordinary: with the cameraphone, tourism begins at home.

While conventional tourist photography, like the postcard, notoriously elides unattractive, polluted, litter-strewn, diseased, or falling-apart sites to capture (and create) a kind of 'staged authenticity' (MacCannell, 1999), cameraphone photography – because of its ease, speed, inexpensiveness, and the very ephemerality of each image – allows for a broader inclusiveness. Not-so-picturesque scenes, oddities, things that are broken or disturbing or provide ironic comment on the aesthetics of the tourist experience itself, are easily consumed and sent – and just as easily deleted. The cameraphone is a furtive weapon that enables its user, the tourist-flâneur-photographer, 'to travel, arrive, gaze, move on, be anonymous in a kind of liminal zone ... to confront the unexpected, to engage in a kind of counter-tourism ...' (Crawshaw & Urry, 1997, p. 179).

Talismania

In August of 2005, I stood for hours near the *daibutsu*, or Great Buddha, of Kamakura, one of the most striking and oft-photographed sites in Japan. Tourists of all ages approached the gigantic bronze statue, gazing up with the astonishment that comes at seeing something so stark and massive and corporeal – and finally viewing in person something seen so many times in pictures. There were tourists armed with all sorts of cameras, digital and otherwise, but many carried only a keitai (Figure 3).

Figure 3. Tourists at the Kôtokuin temple in Kamakura photographing the Great Buddha.

They duly snapped pictures, sometimes of the Buddha on its own, sometimes with family or friends posing in front of it.

What happens when something so inexpressively monumental as the Great Buddha is apprehended within the confines of a keitai's miniature screen (Figure 4)? The gargantuan body of the statue is reduced to a tiny two-dimensional sign and the mode of interaction is reversed – that which the tourists gazed up at in awe is now held in the palm of the hand, gazed down upon. It is an instant souvenir, akin to a postcard or the miniature replicas of the statue sold nearby, authenticating the visit and completing Urry's 'hermeneutic circle'. It also becomes a kind of talisman, like the *omamori* or good luck charms sold by the temple itself (Okabe & Ito, 2006, p. 90). A potent form of sympathetic magic – both homeopathic and contagious – is operating here, for the viewer has not only created a personalized replica of the sight, but that replica is all the more powerful for having been (digitally) extracted from the actual site. Like any photograph, but perhaps more so, a cameraphone image operates as 'a trace, something directly stenciled off the real, like a footprint or a death mask' (Sontag, 1977, p. 154). Through its facile appropriation, the tourist-place becomes commonplace, the remarkable thing becomes a parcel of the everyday, carried in the pocket, a new addition to the narrative of the self.

Pedestrian narratives

Ultimately, then, the keitai helps blur distinctions between everyday life and tourism. Urban planner Kevin Lynch long ago suggested that the experience of the city can be understood as a form of reading, considered in terms of its 'legibility' (Lynch, 1960); similarly de Certeau has famously discussed walking through a city as a kind of

Figure 4.   Photographing the Great Buddha.

'speech act', in which the walker appropriates the 'topographical system' (de Certeau, 1984, pp. 97–99). The encounter with any landscape is akin to a rhetorical practice: through an act of 'personal archiving' (Okabe & Ito, 2006, pp. 87–90), a cameraphone user makes critical choices about which sites to read-write. Later, by sharing the appropriated images with others (electronically or in person), s/he creates an 'allusive and fragmentary story whose gaps mesh with the social practices it symbolizes' (Harvey, 1990, pp. 213–214). Such acts of 'self-expression' and 'self-presentation' are often performed in a social setting, the visual images fleshed out and explained through an (often) oral recounting (Van House et al., 2004).

The narrativizing of images in the social context once more makes traditional distinctions between the extraordinary and the everyday, between being a tourist and going about your daily activities, less and less relevant. Sights are recontextualized – a boyfriend's face followed by a monumental bronze Buddha – leveling out all things great and small. Similarly, public and private are shuffled together; on snapping the photo the individual becomes personally invested in the collective experience of an event or place. The keitai serves as a portable miniature photo album of the latest trip, the latest baby pictures, or the latest party. It extends memory, visually bolstering oral narrative. And such photos, these intimate glimpses into the world of the narrator, are often shared in a personal almost conspiratorial fashion, as several people gather around the screen, looking down, smiling, laughing – a kind of play that glistens with the excitement of passing notes behind the teacher's back.

Flower viewing

The pink blossoms of the cherry tree, or *sakura*, are historically associated with a supposed Japanese taste for short-lived beauty, for the thing that blooms gloriously, delicately, and then, with the gentlest breeze, floats to the ground. To celebrate this precious, ephemeral existence, drunken raucous parties are held throughout the country. Critical for planning these 'flower-viewing' (*hanami*) events is knowing exactly when the cherries will bloom in your area; in 2007, the agency that was able to forecast this with the most accuracy did so by analysing historical trends and current weather conditions, but most importantly by receiving data from 4000 cherry tree observers stationed throughout the country. 'We have people monitor specific trees in their region', a meteorologist explained. 'They send us cell phone picture images on a daily or weekly basis, which gives us a much more accurate picture of how the cherry blossoms are doing in different regions' (quoted in Walsh, 2007). Cameraphones are not just part of the consumption of tourism but have become implicated in its production. Even for party planning, the early twenty-first century requires the 'transfer of information' at, in Paul Virilio's words, 'the absolute velocity of electromagnetic waves' (quoted in Armitage, 2001, p. 27).

Cherry blossoms, synonymous in Japan with the fleetingness of life, are particularly apt as a subject for cameraphones. The effortlessness of cameraphone photography decelerates perception, allowing moments to be stilled, remembered, recounted, rehearsed, re-imagined, re-narrated and held onto indefinitely. As readily as images are captured, however, they are just as easily deleted, erased from digital and, often, neurological memory. There is a schizophrenic interplay here between the fleeting and the permanent; studies have shown that cameraphone users may become 'attached' to photos 'seen at the time of capture as transitory' (Van House, Davis,

Ames, Finn, & Viswanathan, 2005, p. 1856). An ephemeral image captured may inspire an even profounder sense of permanence, as if a fleeting moment has been rescued from the void, and its loss (deletion) is all the more deeply experienced: 'Dropped calls, common with mobile phones, can be re-connected; lost images are irrecoverable' (Van House et al., 2005, p. 1856).

As an emerging technology the cameraphone presents the user with a set of paradoxes revolving around permanence and ephemerality, original and replication, now and then, here and there. The cameraphone itself does not bridge these abstract binaries, but as it becomes more and more an unremarkable tool of everyday life, it suggests that there is nothing contradictory, paradoxical, or cognitively dissonant about them at all. In practice there is a cognitive resonance here: to the tourist-flâneur-photographer the process of deletion and forgetting makes possible the process of recording and remembering.

The medium in which it is accomplished

'During long periods of history', Walter Benjamin says,

> the mode of human sense perception changes with humanity's entire mode of existence. The manner in which human sense perception is organized, the medium in which it is accomplished, is determined not only by nature but by historical circumstances as well. (Benjamin, 1968, p. 222)

Just as the nineteenth-century development of photography went hand-in-hand with the growth of the tourist industry (Crawshaw & Urry, 1997), so technology and the way we perceive and consume tourist sites are indelibly linked. Maybe the cameraphone is nothing more than a particularly convenient way of doing something we have done before: after all, there is nothing new about taking snapshots, admiring them, sharing them with friends, and then stashing them away somewhere to be forgotten. On the other hand, the many tiny changes brought about by cameraphone usage may indeed combine to contribute to a more meaningful shift in 'the mode of human sense perception'. The cameraphone is one small gust of wind (both cause and effect) within a much broader epistemological tempest. We cannot know the extent and profundity of the changes wrought by this storm until the dust settles – if the dust ever settles.

Insufficient 'now'

Way back in 1970, Alvin Toffler, in his bestseller *Future Shock*, warned that 'Even many people who understand intellectually that change is accelerating, have not internalized that knowledge, do not take this critical social fact into account in planning their own personal lives' (Toffler, 1970, p. 21). The way in which cameraphones and other digital technologies are rapidly and unquestioningly incorporated into contemporary life suggests that, in fact, the modernist, evolutionary model Toffler was critiquing no longer obtains. Cameraphone users adopt technology with an almost giddy awareness that it is provisional, that each fantastic new gadget is just one node in an inexorable process. However sleek and functional a just-released technological masterpiece may seem, it will soon be upgraded if not replaced altogether. In such a 'throwaway' society ideas and values and forms of knowledge (expertise, experience, geography) are so short-lived as to be disposable themselves (Toffler, 1970, p. 47; Harvey, 1990, p. 286), a point made almost four decades ago that has only become increasingly salient as wireless technology pervades the marketplace.

New products/techniques are produced, consumed, upgraded, and retooled with a dizzying rapidity. Google, that reliable old search engine, came on line barely a decade ago. YouTube started in 2005, Flickr in 2004. The pace of change accelerates and the number of new practices, and reinvented old ones, increases each day. There is, as Hegel suggested, a point at which quantitative change becomes qualitative change, a mechanism that applies not only to scientific phenomena (e.g., the transformation of water into steam as heat increases), but can also explain 'categorical changes in social evolution' (Carneiro, 2000, p. 12927). With the cameraphone, time and space may not be compressed into nothingness but they have moved qualitatively closer. As the pace and quantity of change accelerates, each moment becomes shorter and shorter – the ease with which photos can be taken, shared, and deleted is part and parcel of an emerging consciousness that may be related to previous practices of photography and tourism but is also qualitatively distinct from those practices.[5]

'Volatility and ephemerality', notes David Harvey (1990, p. 291), 'make it hard to maintain any firm sense of continuity'. How does one negotiate this volatility? 'We have no idea, now, of who or what the inhabitants of the future might be', explains global entrepreneur Hubertus Bigend, a character in William Gibson's novel, *Pattern Recognition*:

> In that sense, we have no future. Not in the sense that our grandparents had a future, or thought they did. Fully imagined cultural futures were the luxury of another day, one in which 'now' was of some greater duration. For us, of course, things can change so abruptly, so violently, so profoundly, that futures like our grandparents' have insufficient 'now' to stand on. We have no future because our present is too volatile.

He goes on to note, 'We have only risk management. The spinning of the given moment's scenarios. Pattern recognition' (Gibson, 2003, pp. 58–59).[6]

The age of digital reproduction as a work of art

To be sure, we can recognize patterns in the way cameraphones are incorporated into common tourist practices in Japan: now practically everybody, regardless of intention, takes a camera along on the tour. But these patterns are unstable. The entrepreneurial producer, like Gibson's Bigend, must capitalize on momentary trends. Tactical flexibility and short-term planning become, in one more oxymoronic marriage, the only viable long-term strategy.

There is labor here for the consumer as well. The tourist-flâneur-photographer does not just make do with the product as given, or use it in the prescribed manner, but works to tease out its secret potential and hidden powers. Cameraphones are increasingly, as de Certeau might put it, 'objects manipulated by practitioners who have not produced them' (de Certeau, 1984, p. 32). Whether complicit, resistant, ideological, playful or benign, such productive consumption is a form of art, a tactical manipulation that may then be co-opted by producers seeking profitable future products and applications (Van House et al., 2004).

Anthropologist Robert L. Carneiro points out that 'the notion of a build-up of quantitative changes until they reach a certain magnitude, at which point they give rise to qualitative changes, has repeatedly proved of value in accounting for structural changes in human societies' (Carneiro, 2000, p. 12930). In the final analysis, the cameraphone may be nothing more than a handy gadget of limited capacity, a new toy that will soon be overwhelmed by fresher technologies and more exciting ways of play. By the same token, though, it may also be an inchoate vehicle through which new meanings are constructed and new social identities forged. It may be the harbinger of not-yet-imagined modes of seeing and knowing, a way to glimpse the glittering thing – whether mundane or spectacular – hidden by the clambering crowd.

Catching a fish

Summer, 2004. Enoshima Aquarium.

It is a sweltering, sweaty Saturday at this aquarium about an hour south of Tokyo. Outside, young couples in designer clothes, wrap-around sunglasses, and white sunhats stroll hand-in-hand. Groups of middle-school students flirt and laugh. Boisterous children yank at the bothered, tired hands of their parents. Inside, it is dark and hot and packed with visitors. Around each smooth, glowing tank, a crowd pushes in to glimpse whatever colorful sea creature is cruising silently inside.

Acknowledgements

This essay first started taking form during a Residential Fellowship at the Center for Ideas & Society at UC Riverside in Fall 2005; I sincerely thank Susan Antebi, Alessandro Fornazzari, and Freya Schiwy for many hours of productive discussion. I am also profoundly grateful to the members of the Shingetsukai Research Group in Japan, particularly Ariga Takashi. My great thanks must also go to the many people, friends and strangers alike, who were willing to talk with me about their own cameraphone use. Finally, the article has benefited immensely from discussion with Ken Rogers, Kenji Tierney, Jason Weems, Jerry Foster and especially, as always, Michiko Suzuki.

Notes

1. Just a quick glance at recent monographs reveals, not surprisingly, that there is also interplay between corporate interests and academic research. Plant (2001) was commissioned by Motorola; Ling (2004) acknowledges the patronage of Telenor, a major European provider of mobile communications services; Ishino (2008) is published by SoftBank Creative, an affiliate of SoftBank Mobile; Kohiyama (2005) is published by NTT Publishing, part of Japanese telecommunications giant NTT, the parent company of NTT DoCoMo, the largest mobile operator in Japan; and Glotz, Bertschi and Locke thank T-Mobile International for being a 'wise and unobtrusive sponsor' (2005, p. 10).
2. Language to signify the device in question is not standardized. Here I choose to invoke a single word, 'cameraphone', in order to emphasize the inseparability of the component parts as well as the integrity of the combination they form.
3. *Chicago Tribune* columnist Clarence Page coined the phrase in an editorial on 12 May 2004. See Jardin (2004).
4. For a litany of the nefarious ways cameraphones have recently been employed, see Agger, 2007. For an example of cameraphones being deployed for resistant surveillance, see www.hollaback.nyc.blogspot.com/
5. In a similar vein, the fact that many of the statistics and observations in this essay may already seem out of date reflects a qualitative shift with regard to traditional academic print

publication, which is becoming – at least when it concerns digital technologies – an expressive mode from a different time zone.
6. Published in 2003, Gibson's novel revolves around a series of online video clips called the 'footage'. Gibson himself comments on how his text documents a moment that is already part of history: 'I'm very grateful that it came out in this tiny remaining window before the emergence of YouTube, which would have changed the whole meaning of the book. People are probably reading it today and thinking, 'Whoa, what happened to YouTube, this is an alternate universe'. I always like to imagine a 12-year old reading 'Neuromancer', getting 20 pages in and turning to his friend and going, 'I figured out what the mystery is! What happened to all the cellphones?'' (quoted in Lim, 2007).

References

Agar, J. (2003). *Constant touch: A global history of the mobile phone.* Cambridge: Icon Books.
Agger, M. (2007, January 17). The camera phone: The gadget that perverts, vigilantes, and celebrity stalkers can all agree on. *Slate.* Retrieved 28 September 2007 from http://www.slate.com/id/2157736/.
Armitage, J. (Ed.). (2001). *Virilio live: Selected interviews.* London: Sage Publications.
Barthes, R. (1981). *Camera lucida: Reflections on photography.* R. Howard (Trans.). New York: Hill & Wang.
Benjamin, W. (1968). *Illuminations.* H. Zohn (Trans.). New York: Schocken Books.
Carneiro, R. (2000, November 7). The transition from quantity to quality: A neglected causal mechanism in accounting for social evolution. *Proceedings of the National Academy of Science, 97*(23), 12926–12931.
Cohen, J. (2005, July 18). Armed with right cellphone, anyone can be a journalist. *The New York Times,* p. C3.
Crawshaw, C., & Urry, J. (1997). Tourism and the photographic eye. In C. Rojek & J. Urry (Eds.), *Touring cultures: Transformations of travel and theory* (pp. 176–195). London & New York: Routledge.
Crouch, D., & Lübbren, N. (2003). Introduction. In D. Crouch & N. Lübbren (Eds.), *Visual culture and tourism* (pp. 1–20). Oxford & New York: Berg.
de Certeau, M. (1984). *The practice of everyday life.* S. Rendell (Trans.) Berkeley: University of California Press.
de Certeau, M. (1992). *The mystic fable, volume one: The sixteenth and seventeenth centuries.* M. B. Smith (Trans.). Chicago: University of Chicago Press.
Fujikawa, D. (2008). *Keitai sekai no kodomotachi* [Children of the keitai world]. Tokyo: Kodansha gendai shinsho.
Fujimoto, K. (2005). The third-stage paradigm: Territory machines from the girl's pager revolution to mobile aesthetics. In M. Ito, D. Okabe & M. Matsuda (Eds.), *Personal, portable, pedestrian: Mobile phones in Japanese life* (pp. 77–101). Cambridge: MIT Press.
Gibson, W. (2003). *Pattern recognition.* New York: Berkley Books.
Glotz, P., Bertschi, S., & Locke, C. (Eds.). (2005). *Thumb culture: The meaning of mobile phones for society.* Verlag, Bielefeld: Transcript.
Goggin, G. (2006). *Cell phone culture: Mobile technology in everyday life.* London & New York: Routledge.
Harvey, D. (1990). *The condition of postmodernity: An enquiry into the origins of cultural change.* Cambridge, MA: Blackwell.
Ishino, J. (2008). *Keitai chirudoren: Kodomotachi wa naze keitai denwa ni botto suru no ka?* [Keitai children: Why are children so absorbed by cell phones?] Tokyo: Sofuto banku shinsho.
Ito, M. (2005). Introduction: Personal, portable, pedestrian. In M. Ito, D. Okabe & M. Matsuda (Eds.), *Personal, portable, pedestrian: Mobile phones in Japanese life* (pp. 1–16). Cambridge: MIT Press.
Ito, M., Okabe, D., & Anderson, K. (forthcoming). Portable objects in three global cities: The personalization of urban spaces. In R. Ling & S. Campbell (Eds.), *The mobile communication research annual volume 1: The reconstruction of space & time through mobile*

communication practices. Transaction Books. Draft retrieved 5 October 2007 from http://www.itofisher.com/mito/portableobjects.pdf.

Jameson, F. (1991). *Postmodernism, or, the cultural logic of late capitalism.* Durham: Duke University Press.

Japan.internet.com. (2006, June 1). Keitai denwa no kamera 77% ga 'hitsuyô', baakôdo yomitori wa hansû ga shiyô [77% say cell phone cameras are 'necessary'; barcode readers used by half of respondents]. Retrieved 1 October 2007 from http://japan.internet.com/research/20060601/1.html.

Jardin, X. (2004, May 26). Wartime wireless worries Pentagon. *Wired.* Retrieved 6 October 2007 from http://www.wired.com/politics/law/new/2004/05/6304.

Kameyama, C. (Producer), & Baba, Y. (Director). (2007). *Babaru e go!! Taimu mashin wa doramu shiki* [Bubble fiction: boom or bust] [Motion picture]. Japan: Toho Company.

Kanellos, M. (2007, April 3). Who invented the camera phone? It depends. *CNET News. com.* Retrieved 28 September 2007 from http://www.news.com/Who-invented-the-camera-phone-It-depends/2010-1041_3-6172586.html.

Kato, F., Okabe, D., Ito, M., & Uemoto, R. (2005). Uses and possibilities of the Keitai camera. In M. Ito, D. Okabe & M. Matsuda (Eds.), *Personal, portable, pedestrian: Mobile phones in Japanese life* (pp. 300–310). Cambridge: MIT Press.

Kato, H. (2005). Japanese youth and the imagining of keitai. In M. Ito, D. Okabe & M. Matsuda (Eds.), *Personal, portable, pedestrian: Mobile phones in Japanese life* (pp. 103–119). Cambridge: MIT Press.

Katz, J. E., & Aakhus, M. (Eds.). (2002). *Perpetual contact: Mobile communication, private talk, public performance.* Cambridge: Cambridge University Press.

Kohiyama, K. (2005). *Keitai no shinkaron* [Evolutionary theory of the keitai]. Tokyo: NTT Shuppan.

Lash, S., & Urry, J. (1994). *Economies of signs and space.* London: Sage.

Lim, D. (2007, Aug. 11). Now romancer. In *Salon.com.* Retrieved 6 October 2007 from www.salon.com/books/int/2007/08/11/william_gibson/?source=newsletter.

Ling, R. (2004). *The mobile connection: The cell phone's impact on society.* San Francisco: Morgan Kaufmann (Elsevier).

Lynch, K. (1960). *The image of the city.* Cambridge: MIT Press.

MacCannell, D. (1999). *The tourist: A new theory of the leisure class.* Berkeley: University of California Press.

Matsuda, M. (2005). Discourses of *keitai* in Japan. In M. Ito, D. Okabe & M. Matsuda (Eds.), *Personal, portable, pedestrian: Mobile phones in Japanese life* (pp. 19–39). Cambridge: MIT Press.

McEwan, I. (2005). *Saturday.* New York: Anchor Books.

Miyaki, Y. (2005). Keitai use among elementary and junior high school students. In M. Ito, D. Okabe & M. Matsuda (Eds.), *Personal, portable, pedestrian: Mobile phones in Japanese life* (pp. 279–299). Cambridge: MIT Press.

Moore, G. E. (1965, April 19). Cramming more components onto integrated circuits. *Electronics, 38*(8), 114–117.

Noguchi, Y. (2005, July 8). Camera phones lend immediacy to images of disaster. *Washington Post.* Retrieved 5 October 2007 from http://www.washingtonpost.com/wp-dyn/content/article/2005/07/07/AR2005070701522.html.

Okabe, D., & Ito, M. (2003, August 29). Camera phones changing the definition of picture-worthy. *Japan Media Review.* Retrieved 28 September 2007 from http://www.ojr.org/japan/wireless/1062208524.php.

Okabe, D., & Ito, M. (2005). Keitai in public transportation. In M. Ito, D. Okabe & M. Matsuda (Eds.), *Personal, portable, pedestrian: Mobile phones in Japanese life* (pp. 205–218). Cambridge: MIT Press.

Okabe, D., & Ito, M. (2006). Everyday contexts of camera phone use: Steps toward techno-social ethnographic frameworks. In J. R. Höflich & M. Hartmann (Eds.), *Mobile communication in everyday life: Ethnographic views, observations and reflections* (pp. 79–102). Berlin: Frank & Timme.

Okada, T. (2005). Youth culture and the shaping of Japanese mobile media. In M. Ito, D. Okabe & M. Matsuda (Eds.), *Personal, portable, pedestrian: Mobile phones in Japanese life* (pp. 41–60). Cambridge: MIT Press.

Parks, B. (2000, October). The big picture. *Wired, 8*(10). Retrieved 28 September 2007 from http://www.wired.com/wired/archive/8.10/kahn.html.

Plant, S. (2001). On the mobile: The effects of mobile phones on social and individual life. Retrieved 5 October 2007 from http://www.motorola.com/mot/doc/0/234_MotDoc.pdf.

Rivière, C. (2005). Mobile camera phones: A new form of 'being together' in daily interpersonal communication. In R. Ling & P. E. Pederson (Eds.), *Mobile connections: Re-negotiation of the social sphere* (pp. 167–185). London: Springer.

Rojek, C., & Urry, J. (1997). *Touring cultures: Transformations of travel and theory.* London & New York: Routledge.

Sontag, S. (1977). *On photography.* New York: Farrar, Straus & Giroux.

Steinbock, D. (2005). *Mobile marketing: The making of mobile services worldwide.* London: Kogan Page.

Toffler, A. (1970). *Future shock.* New York: Random House.

Toyota Motor Sales. (2004). *05 Corolla.* Toyota Motor Sales, USA, Inc.

Urry, J. (2002). *The tourist gaze* (2nd ed). London: Sage Publications.

Van House, N., & Davis, M. (2005). The social life of camera phone images. In *Workshop on pervasive image capture and sharing: New social practices and implications for technology workshop at the seventh international conference on ubiquitous computing in Tokyo, Japan.* Retrieved 5 October 2007 from http://www.people.ischool.Berkeley.edu/ ~vanhouse/Van%20House,%Davis%20%20The%20Social%20Life%20of%20Camera%20Phone%20I-mages.pdf.

Van House, N., Davis, M., Takhteyev, Y., Ames, M., & Finn, M. (2004). The social uses of personal photography: Methods for projection future imaging applications. Working paper. Retrieved 6 October 2007 from http://www.people.ischool.Berkeley.edu/ ~vanhouse/van%20house_et_al2004b%20.pdf.

Van House, N., Davis, M., Ames, M., & Viswanathan, V. (2005). The uses of personal networked digital imaging: An empirical study of cameraphone photos and sharing. In *Extended abstracts of the conference on human factors in computing system (CHI 2005)*, pp. 1853–1856. Portland: ACM Press.

Walsh, B. (2007, March 20). Global warming is hell on party planners. *Time.* Retrieved 6 October 2007 from http://www.time.com/time/world/article/0,8599,1601110,00.html.

A stock market theory of culture: a view from the Latin American neoliberal transition

Alessandro Fornazzari

Department of Hispanic Studies, University of California Riverside, USA

Comparatively focusing on the cultural representations of two historic stock market crashes (fin de siècle Argentina and Chile in the early 1980s), this article explores the stock market theory of value that emerges out of a reactionary nineteenth century critique of exchange value and the so-called new economic paradigm based on information technology.

This essay explores a historical transition in the concept of abstraction. Abstraction, in the context of the Southern Cone neoliberal transition, refers to the commodity logic of finance capital and the specific focus will be on its embodiment in the figure of the stock market. This transition will be made visible through a comparative examination of a nineteenth century model of commodity abstraction which I explore using an Argentinean stock market novel *La Bolsa* (*The Stock Market*) and a radically transformed logic of abstraction that emerges a century later in Chile where financialization intensifies with the advances in computer power and information networks. This comparison brings into focus some of the differences between a classically liberal export-oriented economic model (Argentina in the 1890s) and one of the model cases of neoliberal economic experimentation (Chile in the 1990s).

As a starting point, I begin with a classic, but still relevant, materialist approach that attempts to conceptually map the relation between literary realism and the role of money in social life: I am referring here of the work of diverse thinkers such as Georg Lukács, Arnold Hauser, and Fredric Jameson among others.[1] This kind of mapping explores the effects that an increase in commerce has had on society by focusing on the emergence of new kinds of perceptions and sensibilities. For example, the realist's investment in the physical properties of objects is purportedly explained by the emergence and expansion of the logic of exchange value. Exchange value's equivalence of objects (based on the money form as the universal equivalent) is what leads to the realistic interest in the body of the world and the dynamic human relationships developed by trade and commerce. As the story goes, in a nascent, bourgeois, commerce-centered society, where the market is the focus of human activity and interaction, both merchants and consumers take a keen interest in the sensory nature of the wares that are being inspected, bought, and sold. The back and forth of barter and trade explains the realist's interest in the psychological and characterological traits of their interlocutors. All this results in new forms of perceptions, ways of seeing, and behavior that ultimately create the conditions for realistic forms of art. This simplification of an orthodox materialist approach highlights some of its determinist characteristics (mechanistic causal linkages, for example), but more to the point it highlights the status that exchange value has as one of economic modernity's central concepts.[2]

In Fredric Jameson's version of this process (1998), the realist moment is understood as one stage in a more general dialectic of secularization and reification. Instead of insisting on a radical break between realism and modernism, Jameson argues that realism should be understood as a kind of modernism in its own right. It contains within itself many of the qualities usually associated with modernism: it is subversive, critical, destructive, and it clears away the useless and jumbled monumentality of older cultural forms (Jameson, 1998, p. 120). Realism does this by seizing on the properties, subjectivities, institutions and forms of an older pre-capitalist life world and stripping them of their hierarchical and religious content. From this standpoint, modernism is not so much an overcoming of realism, but an intensification of the processes of reification already at work in realism. The modernist difference is that these processes are intensified to such a point that they end up cannibalizing the realist form. Thus some of the basic ideological preconditions of realism, such as the belief in a stable social reality, are unmasked, demystified, and ultimately discredited. In this way, Jameson puts the realism/modernism debate within the broader context of a transition from one mode of production to another while stressing that these transitional moments are themselves always part of a permanent struggle between coexisting modes of production. It is within this transitional logic that I want situate *La Bolsa*'s realist critique of speculative accumulation.

La Bolsa was published in 1890 in the Buenos Aires newspaper *La Nación* by Julián Martel (a pseudonym of José María Miró). The novel delivers a moralistic critique of the emerging materialist culture around the time of the 1890 economic crash in Argentina. This crash was precipitated by the sovereign debt crisis known as the Baring crisis. Attracted by friendly international investment policies that were put in place by the Argentinean state, the London-based financial firm Baring Brothers had invested heavily in Argentina in the 1880s. With the rise of interest rates at home, the company went into financial crisis and had to be bailed out by the Bank of England. The resulting disinvestment contributed to the collapse of the Argentinean economy in 1890.[3] One of the historical significances of the crisis is that it raised serious questions about the liberal export-led development model; Argentina eventually recovered from this crisis and export-led development continued until the crash of 1930 after which there was a transition to import-substitution industrialization. In this sense the Baring crisis can be said to prophetically announce a coming demise.

La Bolsa fictionalizes the 1890 period of financial instability and is a profoundly anti-Semitic and anti-immigrant text that maintains a consistent and shrill lament against 'those parasites of our wealth that immigration brings from remote faraway places' (Martel, 1956, p. 11).[4] The novel's central figure, the stock market – repeatedly characterized as a corrupting and Jewish space – is portrayed as vampiric in nature: it represents the abandonment of a regime of accumulation based on the values of work and production, and the transition to a regime of market speculation based on illusion, delusion, and chicanery. The stock market appears in the novel as a space of radical contamination: a promiscuity of languages, social mobility, the mixing of high and low, of the tragic and the comic, and of the grotesque and the dramatic. The stock market comes to represent an 'anti-aesthetic and curious showcase' (Martel, 1956, p. 11), which ultimately produces traitors to the *patria* (fatherland). I contend that the racist and reactionary critique of materialism (portrayed simplistically and moralistically in the novel as the selfish preoccupation with goods and money) that the novel deploys is a reaction by a residual class formation against the dematerializing logic of abstraction associated with the cycles of finance capitalism. In the novel these are characterized by the constant fear of the degeneration of petty bourgeois values: the family, the nation, and traditional gender roles.

Jean-Joseph Goux's work on value and the stock market is useful for understanding this transition that Martel's novel is reacting against (1997). For Goux, the logic of the stock exchange undoes some of the major oppositions of modern thought. It unravels the distinctions between the true and the fictitious, the real and the unreal, the act and its simulacra. It is anti-rationalist, it is capitalism at its peak, but it exceeds rational calculation. This according to Goux confounds a whole tradition of critical thinking that has understood calculating reason as a dominant and alienating form of thought inherent to capitalism (Weber, Lukács, Horkheimer among others). When dealing with stock shares what matters is not the 'real' value at a certain moment, but rather what it will be further down the line. What is at the heart of this regime of accumulation is a speculation on difference. The old stalwarts of stability and invariability do not produce profit, on the contrary, big fluctuations in prices do. Profit-making takes place by gambling on wide margins of fluctuating differences. This kind of speculation takes place without the presence of goods or payments. Goods can be sold, purchased, and resold over and over again without the dealers ever physically exchanging them. It is only the difference that is being passed on; the merchandise is being rendered immaterial. As the banknote replaced the circulation of precious metals, an even more abstract and complex form of currency, credit, now moves in. The kind of abstraction associated with this form of currency – what Giovanni Arrighi calls second order abstraction – is of a different order from the exchange value abstraction that supported realism's interest in the physical properties of objects. The logic of financial speculation (that is the paradigm of investment, risk, fluctuation values, and profit margins) places a premium on novelty, anticipating trends, identifying and interpreting indicators, on performing in a highly subjective and often arbitrary medium. For Goux the two figures that emerge as most in tune to this logic of financial speculation are the aesthetic avant-garde and the fashion industry. Both are integrally linked to a gambling on novelty, surprise and difference. Two of the major targets of *La Bolsa*'s reactionary critique are the fashion industry (how the importation of specifically French fashion is diluting the moral fabric of Argentinean women) and cosmopolitanism (immigration as contagion). The novel's interest in the sensuous nature of the world, psychological and characterological traits, and the dynamic relationships developed by trade and commerce all serve to decry the degenerative effects (political, ethical, and aesthetic) that the logic of financial speculation introduces into the national space. In this sense *La Bolsa* in a residual cultural formation whose critique of Argentina's export-led model of economic modernity, which privileges the forms of abstraction associated with exchange value, nostalgically harkens back to a previous regime of accumulation.

If Julián Martel's late nineteenth century stock market novel can be understood as a reaction against the undermining of some of the basic ideological preconditions of realism by the speculative logic of finance capital, then I want to argue that one hundred years later Arturo Fontaine Talavera's 1990 stock market novel, *Oír su Voz* (*Hear Her Voice*), articulates a different critique and reacts to a different form of abstraction. The context out of which Fontaine Talavera's novel emerges concurs with an epochal turning point in Chilean history and in the history of neoliberalism: the transition from one regime of accumulation to another and the transformation of Chile into one of the modern laboratories of neoliberal economic experimentation. This epochal transition names the passage from a traditional oligarchic and agrarian order to full-blown neoliberal capitalism initiated by the modernizing reforms of the Eduardo Frei Montalva (1964–70) and Salvador Allende (1970–73) periods, which are then rechanneled and radically intensified during the dictatorship (1973–89) and *Concertación* (1989 to the present) periods.

Oír su Voz is saturated with the discourse of financial investment. It fills pages and pages with the specialized language of monetarism (stocks, bonds, IVA (value added tax), interest rates, TIR (internal rate of return), land speculation, debt, and credit). The reader is immersed in the world of private companies, the stock exchange, *Banco de Chile* functionaries, and a group of entrepreneurs centered around the *Banco Agrícola e Industrial* (a small bank nationalized during the Popular Unity period and then privatized during the dictatorship). The narrative is also intercalated with advertising clips, television executives' pitches for advertising campaigns, and the descriptive labels of commodity items such as sun tanning lotion. This saturation of the discourse of political economics, where even the characters function as abstract economical conceptualizations, signals the economization of life under neoliberalism. The central conflict that the novel attempts to resolve can be framed as the neutralization of the tensions and contradictions that emerge as a new notion of abstraction (modeled on the stock market and represented by a new breed of financial entrepreneur) subsumes older forms (represented by displaced hacienda owners who are still haunted by their agrarian past).

The historical event that haunts *Oír su Voz* is the agrarian reform. More so than the 1973 military coup, the agrarian reform's shadowy presence pervades the novel, seemingly constituting something like its master code or ultimately determining instance. In the novel, the protagonist's (Pelayo Fernandez) family owned a large country estate (*fundo*) that was expropriated during the Popular Unity's period of agrarian reform. Then, not uncharacteristically, during the dictatorship it was not returned to its previous owners, but parceled up and auctioned off. In the Chilean case, it was this kind of economic policy (quite accurately represented in the novel) that permitted modern agribusinesses to move into the region and ultimately resulted in the genesis of the agricultural boom. In *Oír su Voz*, the result is that the Fernandez family is displaced from the countryside. This particular family's experience is then put into a more general historical picture, which takes into account the profound social and economic transformations that took place in the wake of the reform. The ironic reference to the old Marquis as a residual figure surviving a transition that has not yet effectively dissolved or incorporated them, evokes the fate of another well known old Marquis in Chilean literature: the Venturas, protagonists of José Donoso's *A House in the Country*. At the end of Donoso's allegorical novel about the 1973 military coup, the surviving Venturas are simultaneously swallowed and preserved in the bowels of their country house, which effectively becomes a secret tomb where they are buried alive. This entombment not only buries them, but also protects them from the deadly thistle storm that announces the end of the reign of the Venturas (characterized by artisanal gold mining and semi-feudal relations of production), and the arrival of foreign investors and multinational capital. In the figure of Pelayo Fernández, *Oír su Voz* resurrects an old Marquis and throws him in the midst of a world utterly transformed by the domination of finance capital over industrial capital. To paraphrase Benjamin's parable on transition, Pelayo is part of a generation that has awakened after a long night and 'now stood under the open sky in a countryside in which nothing remained unchanged but the clouds' (Benjamin, 1969, p. 84). Along with the change in landowners and crops, the novel describes the changing labor practices that begin to emerge after the agrarian reform. What is emphasized in this change is not just the loss of land and customs, but, for better or for worse, the loss of a whole way of life, and with it the hegemony of a sector of Chilean society that for much of its history has held enormous political and economic power. In *Oír su Voz*, the agrarian reform stands in for what under different headings (the great transformation, the long delayed transition, the capitalist revolution or counter-revolution) has been described as the passage from the old oligarchic and agrarian order to the modern era.

The agrarian reform (initiated during Eduardo Frei Montalva's Christian Democratic government in 1967) definitively ended the *latifundio* system, and radically altered the Chilean landscape (it affected practically all cultivated lands).[5] After the military coup, with the exception of a limited number of cases, the expropriated lands were not returned to the previous owners. Part of the land, the reserve, was left to the old proprietors; a majority of it was delivered to the peasants who worked it; and a part was auctioned off to large forestry companies and medium sized modern agribusinesses (Riesco, 1989, p. 32). Besides a decline in the number of people employed in agriculture and a sharp climb in urbanization, the most profound effect of this was the creation of a market in land that exploded the static agricultural structure based on the *latifundio* system. Thus, the transition was accelerated by the agrarian reform. Its modernizing potential was then appropriated and re-canalized by the dictatorship (stripped of the social benefits and provisions established during the socialist Popular Unity period). Javier Martínez and Arturo Díaz have pushed this argument the farthest. They argue that the decade of progressive reforms (1964–73) and the 17 years of neoliberal reforms (1973–90) were led not by markets or civil society, but rather by the state and by elites firmly rooted in it. Although the 1964–73 reforms had an entirely different orientation from the neoliberal reforms, there are important elements of continuity between the two periods. One of the specific or exceptional characteristics of the Chilean transition is that the implementation of structural reforms (the economic 'shock' plan of 1975) preceded the adoption of this economic ideology by the International Monetary Fund and World Bank as their official policy toward Latin America. It was only after the 1983 external debt crisis that these two institutions became more involved in Chile (Martínez & Díaz, 1996, p. 48). This means that narratives that situate the Latin American neoliberal transition within the context of the crisis of the national-populist Keynesian state, catalyzed by the 1982 debt crisis, and the waves of privatizations that swept over Latin America during the 1890s and 1990s, end up erasing all the historical specificity of the Chilean capitalist revolution. For example, in Chile by this period it is almost an anachronism to talk about privatizations because between 1973 and 1990 nearly all the public companies had already been privatized.[6] In contrast to what occurs in other Latin American contexts, there is not a huge influx of immigrants or the conquest of new agricultural land, as in the case of Brazil for example. What is already in motion in Chile in this period is the real subsumption of society under capital. Thus for the Chilean case, neoliberalism – understood here as the putting into practice of the Chicago school's reworking of neoclassical economic doctrine (privatization, flexibilization of labor, 'downsizing' and rationalization, de-regulation and diminished capital market restrictions) – needs to be situated in relation to a longer period of economic and political transformation.

Positing the agrarian reform as doing the work of the transition casts Pelayo Fernandez as vestigial from a prior mode of production. It is not so much that he is a transplant from one regime to the other, but rather he embodies the systemic antagonism born from the coexistence of several modes of production. He is, on the one hand, the slick journalist and advertising executive that is comfortable in all the chic metropolitan spaces. Pelayo circulates between very different social scenes: the world of advertising agencies and catchy jingles, the glass towers of high finance, stuffy board meetings with high ranking state officials, an exclusive old boys network (membership dues require having gone to a prestigious private school), the dilapidated university scene, and kitschy neo-avant-garde performances. Yet on the other hand, he is a displaced, alienated, melancholic, would-be inheritor of a collapsed traditional world. Through Pelayo's vestigial status, the novel articulates the problem of the subsumption of older forms that it will then attempt to resolve. The question is whether Pelayo is an agent that resists assimilation from the new systemic dominant or whether he seeks deliverance from it. The novel's attempt at a resolution to this problem will take a turn through the work of nostalgia and melancholy.

Pelayo has the dubious distinction of representing the new emerging journalism in Chile (which is depicted as both frivolous and witty). He jumps from a glossy magazine to a start up private television channel, and this initiates him into the world of high finance. By focusing on the struggle to privatize television, the novel situates Pelayo in the crux of one of the central conflicts between the Chilean state and the private sector. Since the arrival of television in Chile in the 1960s, its ownership was by law restricted to the state and three universities. Even in the post-1973 era when the official discourse stressed free markets, the pressure to liberalize this monopoly was met with stubborn opposition from the state. *Oir su Voz* restages this power struggle, revealing how dogmatically both groups (the state and the private sector) believed that television was the key to maintaining hegemony.

In the tradition of Balzac's symbolic narratives of class representatives, Fontaine Talavera's novel gives a taxonomical account of this new emerging entrepreneurial class: the infamous 'Chicago boys.' This new emerging entrepreneurial class appears in the novel as displacing politicians, intellectuals, and artists; they are technocrats with PhDs, applying rational choice theory to the whole social field. Their most revolutionary contribution is a new focus on the money form. This monetary emphasis corresponds to what has been described as the neoliberal move from labor to money as the source of value, resulting in a situation where 'money begets money.'

Opposed to this new breed of entrepreneur represented in the novel by characters like Mempo and Aliro Toro is Rubén Eskanazi, who is described as an 'old fashioned Latin American businessman' (Fontaine Talavera, 1992, p. 99). For Mempo, he represents all that is wrong about the business World. Eskanazi is never in debt because he never risks anything. He has no projects in his head that he is passionate about or any new ideas on how to produce wealth. This contrast between the old school businessmen and the young piranhas reveals one of the fundamental transformations that has occurred: traditional bourgeois values (sobriety, thrift, work ethic, calculation, and foresight) no longer correspond to the demands of contemporary capitalism. The kind of petty calculation and expected profit return that structured the world of someone like Rubén Eskanazi, are of little use to the likes Mempo or Aliro Toro, who need to imagine and create a demand before there even is one. Their work takes on the characteristics of creative artistic activity, rather than the cold calculating reason associated with other moments of capitalist accumulation.

A premium is put on anticipating trends, identifying and interpreting indicators, on performing in a highly subjective and often arbitrary medium. It is all about gambling on novelty, surprise, and difference. It is the work of creative artists. Mempo's fall into economic and social ruin at the novel's end is, the reader is led to believe, tied to his rationalist limitations. Although fascinated by the flash and speed of this turbulent new world of high finance, he is unable to let go of his conservative bourgeois inhibitions in order to fully embrace the all or nothing risks of casino capitalism. He remains to the very end, tethered to the illusion of calculability and predictability instilled in him by his economic training. This is, ultimately, the deciding difference between Mempo and Toro, who as the economic wonder child emerges unscathed from each market crisis and economic scandal already planning his investment in the next empire-building venture.

In their article on the neoliberal transition from the state to the market, Pierre Bourdieu and Loïc Wacquant identify two new types of cultural producer who have taken the place of the traditional intellectual: the expert who prepares highly technical documents to justify policy made on non-technical grounds; and the 'communication consultant to the prince' who gives academic veneer to the political projects of the neoliberal state and the business nobility (Bourdieu & Wacquant, 2001, p. 5). The novel's protagonist Pelayo represents another type of neoliberal intellectual whose work consists of aestheticizing the visual culture of consumerism. Yet Pelayo cannot simply be reduced to advertising's logic of commodity aesthetization. His distant, ironic, and aseptic relation to the present hints at an at least latent critical relation to the present. This is most evident during his melancholy moments.

Aliro Toro, the most dynamic and aggressive of the entrepreneurs depicted in the novel, is the antithesis of Pelayo in regards to the latter's melancholy relation to the past. In Toro's case the agrarian reform is not a traumatic event that displaces him from a traditional world, but an opportunity he seizes upon to build an economic empire. To accomplish this he capitalizes on the opening up of land speculation and the agricultural boom. Toro embodies the defining characteristics of an emerging financial elite – he is described in the novel as both a new kind of conquistador – and the emergence of new kinds of perceptions and social relations. Perhaps the most central of these is the category of abstraction as it is configured by finance capital. For example, although his fortunes were built on the agricultural boom, Aliro Toro never visits his vineyards or marine farms. The notion of abstraction that begins to emerge here refers to an emptying of stable substances and their unifying identifications (the different kinds of crops and their value in gold or silver); an immateriality of the commodity (its value is no longer found in itself, in its weight or measure, but like money, its always outside); and the quality of endless transferability. From the cycle of revolutions – the agrarian reform being one of the most important – that led to the collapse of the old oligarchic order, emerges a new capitalist regime that recodifies, under the banner of abstraction, older forms of commodities and commodity relations. Toro's agricultural world is stripped of all the traditional relations once associated with it and emptied of its content.

In its representation of the new political economy, the novel emphasizes the playful, gaming aspect of the stock market, appearing more like the simulacrum of commerce than the actual buying and selling of goods. This playfulness also reveals the anachronistic state that the productivist and utilitarian concepts of political economy find themselves in. The stock market's emphasis on the unpredictable, the undecidable and the aleatory sweep away the old bourgeois values of thrift, sobriety and ascetics. Its model of value is driven by a notion of fundamental instability, the logic of the transferable, the play of speculation, and the free flow of finance. Thus, 'it is no longer the factory but rather the "trading pit" that becomes the sacred place of exchange-value's mysteries' (Goux, 1997, p. 163). If stock-market capitalism is defined by its unpredictability and playfulness, then its workers, Toro and Mempo for example, correspond more to the avant-garde notion of the artist (with its imperative of innovation at any price) than to the traditional notion of the economist.

The other characteristic of the stock market model of value that is central to the novel is the emergence of a new articulation of abstraction. Not only are goods substituted for shares, coins, vouchers, and papers, but these tokens are themselves abstracted and separated from whatever product they may have once represented. This process of abstraction renders the products immaterial, infinitely transferable to any part of the world. In this way speculation takes place in the absence of both goods and payment: kiwis, avocados, and grapes are bought and sold (often repeatedly) without the dealers ever having to touch or see a piece of fruit. What they are really trafficking in is difference. Difference is the engine that fuels this whole speculative process.

What I have been attempting to do in this paper is think about how the concept of abstraction is expressed in expressed in two different historical moments (1890 and 1990). *La Bolsa*, working from a realist tradition that privileges the physical properties of objects (expressing a particular model of exchange value and commerce), is highly reactive to the logics of abstraction associated with the stock market. The emergence of the stock market represents the displacement of the old class order. *Oír su Voz*, on the other hand, is not reactive to, but rather the voice of the logics of abstraction associated with the stock market. It is a novel that gives expression to the idea that to really understand finance capital one needs to leave behind the old utilitarian tools of political economy, and think instead from the perspective of the avant-garde artist (spurred on by innovation at any price) the fashion industry, and concepts of virtuosity. Another way to think about this transition from 1890 to 1990 and the changing concept of abstraction is to compare Hilferding's early 1900s reflections on banks engaging in commodity speculation (wheat, porkbellies, oil, and metals) with the second order abstraction that emerges in the 1990s. In the neoliberal context out of which *Oír su Voz* emerges, speculation not only includes commodities but personal debt, mortgages, currency contracts, corporate securities etc. There was already a logic of abstraction at work in the first moment of commodity speculation, in this second moment there is an abstraction to a second degree.

Notes

1. See, respectively, The Historical Novel, The Social History of Art, and A Singular Modernity.
2. Walter Benjamin's work on Charles Baudelaire's lyrical poetry is the fundamental text here for understanding the cultural characteristics and central place that exchange value has for nineteenth century European modernity.
3. For analyses of the Baring crisis see Victor Bulmer-Thomas (2003) and David Rock (2002).
4. All translations from the Spanish are my own.
5. Latifundismo is a system of land ownership based on large landed estates owned by local gentry, absentee landlords, and domestic or foreign corporations.
6. The copper company CODELCO is an important exception to this project of privatization.

References

Arrighi, G. (1999). *The long twentieth century: Money, power, and the origins of our times.* London: Verso.
Benjamin, W. (1969). The storyteller. In H. Arendt (Ed.), *Illuminations* (pp. 83–109). Trans. H. Zohn. New York: Schocken Books.
Benjamin, W. (2003). On some motifs in Baudelaire. In H. Eiland & M.W. Jennings (Eds.), *Walter Benjamin: Selected writings*, vol. 4 (pp. 313–55). Trans. E. Jephcott and others. Cambridge: Belknap Press of Harvard University Press.
Bourdieu, P., & Wacquant, L. (2001). Neoliberal newspeak: Notes on the new planetary vulgate. *Radical Philosophy, 108*, 2–7.
Bulmer-Thomas, V. (2003). *The economic history of Latin America since independence.* Cambridge University Press.
Donoso, J. (1984). *A house in the country.* Trans. D. Pritchard with S.J. Levine. New York: Knopf Inc.
Fontaine Talavera, A. (1992). *Oír su voz [Hear her voice].* Santiago: Planeta.
Goux, J.-J. (1997). Values and speculation: The stock exchange paradigm. *Cultural values, 1*(1), 159–77.
Hauser, A. (1999). *The social history of art.* New York: Routledge.
Hilferding, R. (1981). *Finance capital. A study of the latest phase of capitalist development.* London: Routledge.
Jameson, F. (1998). Culture and finance capital. *The cultural turn: Selected writings on the postmodern, 1983–1998* (pp. 136–161). London: Verso.
Jameson, F. (2002). *A singular modernity: Essay on the ontology of the present.* London: Verso.
Lukács, G. (1983). *The historical novel.* Lincoln & London: University of Nebraska Press.
Martel, J. (1956). *La bolsa [The stock market].* Buenos Aires: Editorial Guillermo Kraft Limitada.
Martínez, J., & Díaz, A. (1996). *Chile: The great transformation.* Washington DC: Brookings Institute.
Riesco, M. (1989). *Desarrollo del capitalismo en Chile bajo Pinochet.* Santiago: Ediciones ICAL.
Rock, D. (2002). Racking Argentina. *New Left Review, 17*, 55–86.

Südländisch: the borders of fear with reference to Foucault

John Namjun Kim

Comparative Literature & Foreign Languages, University of California, Riverside, USA

This article examines the term 'südländisch' in the German news media's description of two suspected terrorists, whose images were captured on video surveillance cameras as they were planting bombs on two German trains in Summer 2006. Strictly untranslatable in just one word, the term *südländisch* is commonly used to designate anyone who appears to come from a 'southern' or Mediterranean country, or simply anyone who appears 'brown.' However, as this article discusses, the video surveillance footage was of such low quality that this description was almost arbitrary. The images of the suspects were not any 'browner' than those of the bystanders whose images were also captured on the video surveillance footage. This article uses the occasion of this medial incident to address the problem of referentiality in Michel Foucault's notion of 'discourse,' showing how the term *südländisch* functions as a discursive formation. Focusing on the borders of discourse as the constitutive moment of discourse, this article then turns to the multiplication and dispersion of borders within the European Union. It argues that the term *südländisch* serves as just one of many borders that have been unwittingly generated by the move toward political integration in the EU.

On 18 August 2006, the German Federal Crime Bureau (BKA) convened a press conference to announce its investigation of a failed bomb attack that was to have taken place some three weeks earlier (BKA, 2006). Two suitcases packed with unconventional explosives set to detonation devices were found on two regional trains prior to explosion. With one train running from Aachen to Hamm and the other from Mönchengladbach to Koblenz, the bombs had traveled through a densely populated region of the country on lines intersecting at Cologne. In the wake of the attacks upon a Madrid commuter train on 11 March 2004 and upon the London Underground on 7 July 2005, the BKA concluded that the German railway was next on the calendar of, what was then feared to be, an annual series of bombings on Europe's transportation network.

However, no sooner than the 'suitcase bomb' incident was announced, what began as a criminal probe of a possible terrorist attack turned into media spectacle centered the interpretation of images, of the visible in the invisible, of mass fear provoked by pixels of light. The video surveillance images of the suspects provided by the BKA to the news media provoked fear less because of what they showed but because of how they were rendered 'legible.' Though these images were of such low quality that neither of the two suspects could be identified beyond their probable gender (male) and probable age group (twenty to forty), they were immediately read as appearing 'südländisch' (see Figure 1).

Strictly untranslatable in just one word, *südländisch* is nevertheless sometimes translated into English as 'southern,' 'tropical,' or 'Mediterranean,' while remaining synonymous with none of these. A term of ambivalence indexing nothing in empirical reality defined in terms of time and space, *südländisch* is a compound adjective derived from the words 'Süden' (south) and 'Land' (land), and is used to suggest the austral origins of a thing or state of affairs. When used to schematize the social, it implies an optic of otherness with the power to condense contraries into one image: images of warmth, plenitude and pleasure overlaid by those of crime, filth and mortal danger. A lens through which bodies were at one time rendered legible as 'Italian' or 'Greek,' *südländisch* today tends to render them legible as 'Turk' or 'Arab.' That is to say, it implies any hue of the human viewed as browned by the southern sun. However phantasmagoric its reality, feint its retinal imprint, or dislocating its identification by terrestrial direction, *südländisch* is how some migrant bodies are seen to refract the light shone upon them into the German public eye, appearing as externalities drawn into the interior, as mere guests to their hosts, or simply as bomb bearing bodies of brown skin.

Yet, in spite of the frequency with which the video surveillance footage was read as depicting *südländisch* subjects, few if any paused to ask to what this designation attests. If the images of the suspects did not appear any 'browner' than the bystanders in the footage – and they did not – how is it that they came to be viewed as appearing *südländisch*? Why would a cluster of video pixels come into focus in such a manner? Or, more to the global political present, how might this convergence

Figure 1. *Zweites Deutsches Fernsehen Online.* Retrieved 1 April 2007 from www.zdf.de.

of video surveillance technology, transportation networks and the fear of death by a perceived austral 'threat' be read? No doubt a historical tracing of the rhetoric and image of the *südländisch* appearing person would serve to answer some, or parts of, these questions. Such a tracing might start with the sixteenth-century circumnavigation of the world and its projection of austral images into what would later become the colonial core of Europe, ending with twentieth-century labor migration movements of peoples from the Mediterranean into German-speaking Europe. However, the questions provoked by the images of *südländisch*-appearing subjects in the video surveillance footage ask something else. Insofar as these images are indistinguishable from those purportedly depicting non-*südländisch* appearing subjects, they raise a basic question about the legibility of the illegible or, from a different perspective, the referentiality of that which is supposed to be seamlessly referential, namely, video surveillance footage. While the temptation stands to read this problematic according to the microphysics of power in terms of Michel Foucault's analysis of Jeremy Bentham's panopticon, an approach from a different, yet no less Foucauldian, perspective will be taken here. The convergence of technologies of surveillance, transportation networks and the image of the *südländisch*-appearing attests to a modulation of what Foucault called 'discourse,' but 'discourse' of a specific form, namely, the border. The image of the *südländisch*-appearing subject is both an instance of discourse as well as the border of another, unspoken discourse, that of fear. Locating this border in order to show its multiplication in a political space that declaims its putative disappearance – the European Union – I reformulate the questions above in terms more basic: To what does 'discourse' refer? In responding to it, we shall see how the designation *südländisch* serves as a border.

Reference in discourse

Of Foucault's many idioms, the term 'discourse' remains the most cited yet simultaneously the most fraught, for it appears all encompassing. There are two critiques of Foucault's notion of 'discourse' that frequently arise, in particular, when it is tied to the question of political engagement. Both deal with the constraint that discourse places on the 'reality' of the political. First, it is said that the notion of discourse remains at an order of abstraction at which it refers only to how things are 'thought' or 'talked about,' rather than the things 'in themselves.' For some readers, it appears as a denial of reality itself to speak about the world only on the 'order of discourse.' For others, it appears circular to propose that the body emerges as a discursive object only in conjunction with the discourse on sexuality. Discourse is discourse, according to this epistemic short-circuit. In other words, discourse is imagined as standing apart from the materiality of the world, the 'referents' that emerge through it. Second, Foucault's theory of discourse implies, if not explicitly then at least in method, a strict determinism of social relations. Subjective agency, it is argued, remains entirely – and Foucault would agree – outside of the scope of his concerns. In other words, the strict determinism of discourse appears at odds with the fundamental political critique motivating his work. Underlying both lines of critique is what appears to be an intractable problem or, simply, a fallacious assumption, in his work, namely, if 'man' is indeed 'dead' – that is, if subjective agency is merely a fiction of modernity – then how is political transformation or action possible? How can Foucault effect a politics with his critique of disciplinary societies? Though it is arguably the less interesting critique, focus belongs on the first of these two because it is the methodological precondition for the second.

In spite of Foucault's thorough-going critique of Kant and 'consciousness,' his theory of discourse remains 'Kantian' with respect to it epistemic approach to 'things' in the world. For things to appear as 'things,' they must be schematized as such, that is, made into subjects of predication. Things are 'things' to the extent that they can be attributed qualities and differentiated from other 'things' however minimally. In terms of the video surveillance footage of the *südländisch*-appearing subjects, the circle around the suspect makes explicit what Foucault calls the 'enunciative level,' or that minimal level of discursivity at which something appears as 'given' prior to its schematization but is, in fact, first given at the moment of schematization (see Figure 1). That which appears to us as 'given' is for Foucault an 'enunciated' (*énoncé*), or in its standard English translation, a 'statement.' Foucault writes in the *Archaeology of Knowledge*, 'the enunciated has this quasi-invisibility of the 'there is,' which is effaced in the very thing of which one can say: "there is this or that thing"' (Foucault, 1972, p. 111). The enunciative level is the level at which a thing has been schematized as a topic, a subject that can be predicated as an object illuminating positivity. In the case of the video surveillance images, it is at the enunciative level at which video pixels are seen, not as pixels, but as an image of a human schematized as *südländisch*. The apparent 'givenness' of things, the 'obviousness' with which they appear in all of their inert facticity, is that which effaces their topicalization, which is visually represented in the video surveillance footage by a circle. Yet, inasmuch as it topicalizes, the circle also effaces its enframing force of saying 'there is this or that thing.' The circle effaces itself, for one is not supposed to gaze at the circle, rather one is supposed to gaze at what is inside it, which is in this case a putatively *südländisch*-appearing person.

Nevertheless, it would still appear as if there were not place for referentiality – for the referent whatsoever – in Foucault's notion of discourse. The materiality of the referent appears to remain fundamentally outside of discourse, radically other to it, something that discourse can never 'touch.' However, the very terms of this characterization of discourse misconstrues how it arises. Discourse and the discrete discursive formations that emerge within it are not notions reducible to the factical sense of the copula 'is.' Rather, they are doings that upset the invisibility of thematizing frames, or optics, that bring discursive vision to the sensorium. Thus, a conceptual distinction is made between 'things' as they stand apart from discursive vision and 'objects' schematized by discursive vision:

> What … we wish to do is to dispense with 'things'. To 'depresentify' them. To conjure up their rich, heavy, immediate plenitude, which we usually regard as the primitive law of a discourse that has become divorced from it through error, oblivion, illusion, ignorance, or the inertia of beliefs and traditions, or even the perhaps unconscious desire not to see and not to speak. To substitute for the enigmatic treasure of 'things' anterior to discourse, the regular formation of objects that emerge only in discourse. (Foucault, 1972, p. 47)

An 'object' is more than the 'thing' to which it is thought to belong. To regard something as a 'thing' is to take it for its illusory 'immediacy' that is imagined as temporally prior to its schematization and placement into a relation with other 'things.' A 'thing' is an object stripped from the matrix of its historicity, its embeddedness in and generation of a historical imagination. It is a node without a matrix, which is to say quite literally 'nothing.' The attempt to reach for the plenitude of 'things' would 'succeed' only by ignoring that it is discourse that naturalizes them as 'things.' That is to say, by focusing on 'objects' rather than 'things,' Foucault emphasizes the network of epistemic relations that make objects appear as they do in time.

Yet, this reading does not bring clarity to the haziness of referentiality in Foucault and, by extension, the haziness of the video surveillance images that provoked it. For, as the prior passage suggests, 'things' still are imagined as 'anterior to discourse.' However, attention must be brought to Foucault's exactingly precise language. He refers to the thing's 'rich, heavy, immediate plenitude, which we usually regard as the primitive law of discourse.' But, what is 'rich, heavy, immediate plenitude'? The problematic with which Foucault wrestles here is the separation between representation and the imagined effect of a reality prior to it. In a different yet proximate context, Timothy Mitchell observes that modernity is characterized by its production and reproduction of representations that accrue their force of the real by virtue of mutual re-enforcement of representations:

> Representation always gathers its strength from the way one picture is echoed and confirmed by another, so that each image forms part of a world-encircling web of signification. Yet the effectiveness of this world-as-picture lies not simply in the process of serialization. It lies in the apparent contrast created by images, which are repeatable, serializable, hyperlinked, open to endless imitation, and the opposing effect of an original, of what appears to be the actual nation, the people itself, the real economy. (Mitchell, 2000, p. 19)

Just as with what Mitchell calls 'representations,' discourse has the effect of not only re-enforcing other discourses but also producing the effect of its putative opposite, that of an underlying 'reality.' This, however, is not to suggest that discourse has come to replace the 'real.' Rather, it means that the 'real' is made such by juxtaposition to its discourse. In other words, discourse is never separate or secondary to the 'real' but always constitutive of it, rendering it subject to predication.

It is in this sense then that Foucault moves from the language of the 'referent' to that of the 'referential.' Whereas the 'referent' is a thing in its simple facticity without schematization (i.e. a 'thing'), the 'referential,' Foucault argues, serves a schematic function. A referential is not a thing, but a rule:

> [The enunciated] is linked ... to a 'referential' that is made up not of 'things,' 'facts,' 'realities,' or 'beings,' but of laws of possibility, rules of existence for the objects that are named, designated, or described within it, and for the relations that are affirmed or denied in it. The referential of the enunciated forms the place, the condition, the fields of emergence, the authority to differentiate between individuals or objects, states of things and relations that are brought into play by the enunciated itself; it de?nes the possibilities of appearance and delimitation of that which gives meaning to the sentence, a value as truth to the proposition. (Foucault, 1972, p. 91)

To speak of a referential, rather than a referent, is thus not to jettison the real imagined as anterior to discourse. It is rather to engage with the referent, not as a thing in its immediacy, but as an object that emerges only according to rules of formation. The referential thus points to matrices of relations and their points of discontinuity that allow for distinctions between objects to be made. Hence, in assuming the perspective of discourse over that of an imagined, simple and unproblematic 'reality,' one shifts one's epistemic gaze toward the rupture between discourses and its other. What is at stake at the order of discourse is not so much what appears through it, or emerges by means of it, but the border that constitutes it as a distinct discourse that remains reflected, if rarefied, in other discourses.

The borders of discourse

The image of the *südländisch*-appearing person as a discursive object thus cannot be examined strictly from the perspective of what immediately appears in the image. The image appears *südländisch* only to the extent that a border has been introduced, one between the public eye that views itself as non-*südländisch* and video pixels thought to capture the image of a mortal threat. That is to say, the borders of discourse and the borders circumscribing political communities are thus continuous with one another even as they appear discontinuous. Technologies of surveillance serve to suture them into a continuity, but not in the sense of creating rigid, stable unities. On the contrary, technologies of surveillance lend mobility to the territorial borders of a political community, enabling their oscillation.

However, before asking how borders can be 'mobile' or can 'oscillate,' it should first be asked: What is a border? A border is not infrequently, yet nonetheless misleadingly, imagined as a stable line between two political communities establishing relations of internality and externality. Yet, this imagination of the border erases the temporal character of the border, presenting it as spatially given 'thing' beyond discourse. It ignores the temporality of the border. A border is temporal not so much in the sense that it is a historically determined object. Rather, a border is temporal with respect to the identity of entities it divides, for drawing a border *will have conferred* the identities of that which it divides, just as identifying an entity as distinct from others *will have traced* a border. Étienne Balibar argues,

> to mark out a border is, precisely, to define a territory, to delimit it, and so to register the identity of that territory, or confer one upon it. Conversely, however, to define or identify in general is nothing other than to trace a border, to assign boundaries or borders ... (Balibar, 2002, p. 76)

Hence, the question 'What is a border?' poses a temporally circular problem: one cannot say what it is without also saying what it divides, but in saying what it divides one draws a border. That is to say, one produces what one seeks to define.

This logical paradox in the temporality of the border effects also a logical paradox in its spatiality. Drawing a border, or identifying a territory, would appear to establish a relation of interiority and exteriority, of that which 'belongs' on one side of the border and that which 'belongs' on the other, such as not only territory but also bodies. It would appear to establish a dual and symmetrical relation in which one side 'mirrors' the other, such that what is 'interior' from one side is simultaneously also 'exterior' from the other, and *vice versa*. However, the apparently simple duality and symmetry established by the border masks how the drawing of a territorial border extends the exterior of the border into the interior and projects the interior into the exterior. It is here that we confront the mobility of borders even as they might appear to be fixed to terrestrial coordinates or secured by walls.

By the conventions of political theory, territorial borders mark the event horizon of the sovereign state and its political imaginary. Where they end, so too does the state. Yet, political practice, life itself, has always belied the absolute terms of this imaginary. Even today as states attempt to project the aura of sovereign power by erecting walls along their borders, such massive markers of sovereignty have come to be signs of the opposite. As Wendy Brown (2007) has recently argued, the erection of walls along the sovereign borders of nation-states marks not the strength of national sovereignty, or sheer state power, but its erosion. This erosion is not only expressed in the erection of external, physical walls, but also by the dispersion of the external border into the interior concentrating on one object, migrant labor power. As Sandro Mezzadra and Brett Nielson argue, labor power is a 'commodity unlike any other' because 'the role of borders in shaping markets is particularly pronounced' by 'filtering and differentiation' of those who participate in it (Mezzadra & Nielson, 2008, section 2). But labor power is inextricably tied to the border not only because territorial borders constitute labor markets, but also – and more poignantly – because labor power always comes in the form of living bodies:

> Unlike the case of a table, for instance, the border between the commodity form of labor power and its 'container' must continuously be reaffirmed and retraced. This is why the political and legal constitution of labor markets necessarily involves shifting regimes for the investment of power in life, which lead for example to complicate the clear cut distinction between sovereignty and governmentality. It is also why the dimension of labor struggle that emerges within the constitution of these markets implies a confrontation with the question of the border. It is precisely the relation between labor power and struggle that links the instances of border reinforcing and border crossing that we analyze in different *borderscapes* ... (Mezzadra & Nielson, 2008, section 2)

As Mezzadra and Nielson suggest, borders are mobile precisely because the labor power they regulate is always embodied with life. Thus, to the extent that one can still use the metaphorics of spatial location in describing a border, its 'site' is not, and never has been, at the point at which territorial sovereignty ends. Rather, it has always been there where bodies are found to circulate both across and within territorial borders. Indeed as bodies circulate, so too do borders.

Thus, in one sense, the border literally circulates with bodies in the form of state-issued documentary identification such as the passport, whose historical emergence is directly tied to the emergence of the modern nation-state (Torpey, 2000). The passport is, in effect, a border insofar as it serves as a semiotic of the state's 'embrace' of its members and confers the right of entry into the territory of one's state. However, inasmuch as it serves as a semiotic of one's political membership, it also conversely can serve as the ground for denying one's entry into the territory of another state. Hence, the metaphorical language of the *sans-papiers*, or persons 'without papers,' used to describe migrants entering the EU without authorization is not altogether without the force of reality. In destroying or simply not carrying state-issued documentary identification or passports, the *sans-papiers* frustrate the state's ability to establish their legal right to reside within the territorial boundaries of the state. More precisely, though the term *sans-papier* is used to designate 'illegal migrants,' the actual lack of documentary identification, or literally being 'without papers,' renders it impossible to say on which side of a territorial border a subject 'belongs.' Thus, as John Torpey notes, a secondary regime of border control has emerged, in particular within the EU, based not on documentary evidence but optical (read: 'racial') characteristics:

> ... one of the most important consequences of regional integration in Europe has been a heightened attentiveness to racial distinctions, at least on the part of the guardians of

national borders. If travelers are not routinely required to produce documents demonstrating their nationality, and the continent is perceived by many of its inhabitants, however anachronistically, as 'white,' visible markers thought to signal membership grow in importance as reasons for suspecting that a person may be liable to movement controls as a non-national of a the Community's member states. Skin color, hair, and the other stigmata of racial identity unavoidably move to the fore as means of identifying outsiders. (Torpey, 2000, p. 154)

In this sense then, the emergence of the *südländisch*-appearing body bears witness to more than the instance of racial profiling that it first appears to be. Its emergence testifies to a larger discursive apparatus in which real or imagined physical markers of the body attain the status of a territorial border, regardless of the 'papers' that body might carry. However, just as the body has become a border, so too has an elaborate institutional apparatus for identifying this border *within* the territorial borders of the state.

In 'Globalized-In-Security: The Field and the Ban-opticon,' Didier Bigo argues that a new 'governmentality of unease' has emerged with the transnationalization of the security networks, especially in the European Union (Bigo, 2006, p. 110). This unease arises not due to 'objective' threats to national and international security, such as 'Islamic terrorism,' but by the emergence of globalized security networks themselves, which rely on the imagination of the secure national borders even as the development of these networks bears witness to the impossibility of absolutely policing these borders. While critics of European integration have observed that the lifting of restrictions to move across the internal (national) political borders has merely transformed into a fortification of the external borders of the EU, Bigo argues to the contrary that these borders have not so much moved to the exterior of the EU but have been dispersed and disseminated across a bureaucracy of professionals who police borders simultaneously at the local level and at a distance. Bigo argues that the policing of borders no longer takes place just at the level of the civil servant, who guards borders from afar 'through the visas and the controls in the consulates of the passengers' country of origin' (p. 121), but is also a task that has been privatized, 'downloaded onto the airline companies and the airports who, in turn, subcontract the job to private security companies' (p. 121).

In other words, state security has been deterritorialized and is no longer concentrated on the physical border, but on the movement of peoples and is thus 'less like a rooted practice of herding than a nomadic practice that follows the seasonal migration of populations who are created as the effect of such proactive logics (p. 122). That is to say, what was once imagined as a border separating the exterior from the interior is now more a matrix in which the exterior is integrated into the interior interpenetrating it to the point at which the external border striates what was once considered the 'internal,' 'domestic' space of the nation state. This 'internal' striation of the 'external' border produces social antagonism that the global networks of 'security,' or more properly, insecurity, were installed to seek:

police practice is directed at the surveillance of foreigners or poor ethnic minorities and extends its reach beyond its prior limits of criminal investigation, through pro-active actions that enable the police to pinpoint groups 'predisposed to criminality' according to sociological knowledge. The diagram of the guilty changes: it no longer derives from supposed criminality, but supposed 'undesirability'. (p. 122)

It is in this sense that the transformation of political sovereignty, in particular in the EU, has led to a new optics of security in which borders are no longer tied to territory but to bodies whose physical presence within the 'internal' borders of the state marks its externality. This is a regime of surveillance that Bigo, following but modifying Foucault's reading of Bentham's panopticon, calls the 'Ban-opticon,' or an apparatus for identifying those who are to be excluded, or 'banned.' This play on words is less a rejection of the Foucauldian model of panopticism, as a paradigm of modern institutionality, than an unfolding of its logic in which the aim of political sovereignty is no longer to exercise sovereign control over subjects but to identify subjects who are to be excluded, not from space of sovereign control, but as a demonstration of sovereignty's 'reality.'

Return to the South

While the metaphorics of the global South have been used in critical discourse to mark a site of resistance against the economic and political violence of the 'West' exacted upon the Rest, the discourse of the *südländisch*-appearing body in German social discourse has never been imagined as a site of critical resistance. Rather, it is a precipitate of a collapsing sovereignty that increasingly seeks to buttress itself by multiplying the borders by which it has previously defined itself and projecting them inward upon bodies that travel within them. Video surveillance cameras, identification controls and internal detention centers among other apparatuses thus serve less the purposes of 'security' than the projection of sovereign power where it finds itself in erosion.

As of November 2008, the 'suitcase bomb' affair has been left unresolved as the apprehended suspects await their trial. While it never came to fore as to how the images of these suspects came to be viewed as *südländisch* despite the low grade video images, it can be surmised that it was due to a retroactive ascription. The BKA's initial announcement indicates a telephone number in Lebanon and a package of Lebanese spices were found near the suitcases – that is to say, indices of yet more borders in the interior.

References

Balibar, É. (2002). What is a border? In *Politics and the other scene* (pp. 75–86). London: Verso.

Bigo, D. (2006). Globalized-in-security: The field and the ban-opiticon. In N. Sakai & J. Solomon (Eds.), *Translation, biopolitics, colonial difference* (pp. 109–55). Hong Kong: Hong Kong University Press.

Brown, W. (2007). Porous sovereignty, walled democracy. Lecture presented at the University of California, Irvine, 7 April 2007.

Bundeskriminalamt [BKA]. (2006). Pressemitteilungen 18 August 2006. Retrieved 20 November 2008 from http://www.bka.de/pressemitteilungen/2006/pm180806_2.html#_jmp0_

Foucault, M. (1972). *The archaeology of knowledge and the discourse on language*. New York: Pantheon.

Mezzadra, S., & Nielson, B. (2008). Border as method, or, the multiplication of labor. *Transversal, 6*. Retrieved on 15 October 2008 from http://translate.eipcp.net/transversal/0608

Mitchell, T. (2000). *Questions of modernity*. Minneapolis: University of Minnesota Press.

Torpey, J. (2000). *The invention of the passport: Surveillance, citizenship and the state*. Cambridge: Cambridge University Press.

Is nostalgia becoming digital? Ecuadorian diaspora in the age of global capitalism

Silvia Mejía Estévez

Foreign Languages Department and American Studies Program, The College of Saint Rose, Albany, NY

Focusing on the recent phenomenon of massive Ecuadorian migration to the United States and Europe, this essay explores how digital technologies are changing the experience of displacement, and how nostalgia – the longing for a home and a time left behind – may feel different in this era of global capitalism when, as advertisements posted on immigrant-oriented web sites claim, home is 'just a click away'. Due to the encounter with new technologies intent upon shrinking space and time, nostalgia might be becoming digital – a quest for continuity of space and time through the simultaneity offered by digital technologies. This essay, then, proposes the category of digital nostalgia as a critical tool for analysing the experience of displacement within the contradictory discourses of globalization, which relentlessly sell the erasure of space, distance and borders, while encouraging legal and territorial barriers that prevent the free circulation of people. For Ecuadorian migrant workers, digital technologies have become the terrain of a daily negotiation between the challenges presented by the reality they physically inhabit and those other commitments based in Ecuador. From this perspective, digital nostalgia is about the annihilation of longing through constant and real-time exposure to a home and a time that are never fully left behind. However, digital nostalgia is also about the conscious use of the simultaneity offered by digital technologies to construct an 'effect' of continuity, secure a sense of belonging, and reverse the processes of fragmentation and uprooting encouraged by global capitalism.

In southern Ecuador, three hours from Cuenca, the country's third largest city, sits Pucará, a small town populated mostly by peasants whose major source of income has always been agriculture. Over the course of the last decades the economic and social situation has substantially changed there. Today, you will find only women and old people working in the plots that surround the center of the hamlet. Other than the school children who play every afternoon in the plaza across from the local church, young people – particularly men – seem to have vanished. Decades ago, young men would descend to the coast to find jobs with the transnational mining companies that still operate in southwest Ecuador, but they would always come back to Pucará during the weekends, and get into trouble while spending their salaries in the local cantinas. Today, however, a growing number of young men – and recently women – leave town as soon as they finish high school, if not before graduation. Usually they move to Cuenca, where sooner or later they get in touch with a smuggler (a *coyote* or *coyotero* in the local slang) who will charge their families between 12,000 and 15,000 dollars to bring them illegally to the United States.

From a lifestyle regulated by the rhythms of agriculture, Pucará's people have switched to the monthly pace imposed by the remittances that their young relatives send them from far and away – mostly from the United States, but also from Spain and Italy during recent years. Even the landscape has changed in the hamlet. The traditional small wooden houses are being replaced by huge concrete constructions sitting on the land that had formerly been mortgaged to pay the *coyote*.

There is yet another transformation in Pucará, probably the most intriguing from the point of view of this essay. Over the roof of a small building annexed to the local church, the *Red de Comunicación de la Pastoral Social de Cuenca* – a Catholic non-profit known for its work with migrants and their relatives – recently installed a parabolic antenna. It provides a satellite Internet connection to the *telecentro* (telecommunications center) that opened its doors about four years ago. Regular telephone service arrived in town just a few years before. There are still a limited number of families that own landlines, but they do not use them to call their relatives living abroad because the service is too expensive. In the *telecentro*, however, Pucará's residents get help with opening free email accounts, so that they can write to their relatives or even have videoconferences with them. That is, of course, if they do not already own a cell phone financed through remittances.

Premodern conditions of living overlap with late capitalist high-tech in Pucará, where people living in settlements deprived of access roads can easily make a cell phone call to New York City . . . but still need to walk three hours to get to the local post office. Pucará represents the extremes in a wide range of intertwined phenomena, including international migration, global capitalism, and nostalgia. This essay will focus on the third element, nostalgia, and will use the recent and specific case of massive Ecuadorian migration overseas as a point from which to analyse how contemporary nostalgia, while intrinsically connected with the industrial age and the modern teleology of progress that saw its birth as an 'unprogressive illness', may feel different in this era of global capitalism when, as the advertisements posted on immigrant-oriented web sites claim, home is 'just a click away'. How have new technologies such as the Internet, satellite communication, email, videoconferences, and cell phones changed the experience of being away from home? How is nostalgia being transformed by the irruption of digital technologies intent upon shrinking space and time? If nostalgia is longing for a place and a time left behind, how are we supposed to experience displacement now that we are becoming virtually ubiquitous and never completely inhabit or leave any place? How are we supposed to long for past times now that past and future seem to disappear in the accelerated, simultaneous, and fragmented realities that populate our permanent present? In short, one could say that nostalgia is becoming digital.

The Ecuadorian diaspora

At least three different waves of Ecuadorian migration occurred in the second half of the twentieth century: the migration processes of the 1960s, those of the 1980s and, finally, the massive migration registered between the last years of the 1990s and the beginning of the twenty-first century, all of them marked by times of economic and political distress in Ecuador, crises in the global market, changes in the immigration policies in the settlement countries, and the solidification of Ecuadorian immigrant networks in those countries (Herrera, Carrillo & Torres, 2005, p. 17).

The crisis in the exports of the 'Panama hat' has been associated with the first wave of Ecuadorian migration. Since colonial times, the weaving and commerce of straw hats had become the cornerstone of the economy for the southern provinces of Cañar and Azuay.[1] The hats, produced by peasant weavers scattered in the Andes and then exported to the United States and Europe through networks of mestizo/white middlemen and rich exporters, acquired their famous name when they 'began to be exported for sale to gold miners passing through Panama during the California gold rush of the 1850s' (Kyle, 2000, p. 56). After World War II the United States, Ecuador's best customer, began to import cheaper hats from Japan, China, Italy, and the Philippines. Moreover, by the 1960s, the use of hats was no longer fashionable. The collapse was inevitable for a local economy dependent on these exports. According to David Kyle, in response to the crisis, middle-class exporters and middlemen, as well as peasants connected to the networks of straw hat commerce, followed the 'Panama hat trail' and settled in New York City in the late 1950s and early 1960s.

During the second wave (1980s to mid 1990s), Ecuadorian migration acquires different characteristics: it mostly originates in the southern provinces of Cañar and Azuay, it presents a strong rural character, and it is mainly composed of male migrants (Herrera et al., 2005, p. 17). A steady flow of migration towards the United States had characterized the 1970s, but in the early 1980s the flow increased. Ecuador, like the rest of Latin America, had to confront a new collapse of the economy, this time due to the Debt Crisis.[2] During what has been called the 'lost decade', the national currency was devalued, salaries diminished, and the minimum annual income dropped about 7.6% between 1982 and 1991. Meanwhile, the cost of living increased, interest rates were higher than ever, and the State cut many social programs (Jokisch, 2001, para. 5). No wonder Ecuadorians from those regions that had already established migratory networks in previous decades found their best option to be migration to the United States.

The most recent wave of Ecuadorian migration is set apart from previous ones not only due to its massive numbers. At least three further shifts differentiate the current diaspora from the migratory processes registered in the 1960s and the 1980s: the crisis registered in Ecuador in the late 1990s brought a migratory stream originating mainly in the urban centers; a high percentage of the migrants are women; and the United States no longer is the main destination of Ecuadorian migrants, who now favor Spain and Italy.[3] This last development may seem surprising. Why did the majority of the Ecuadorian diaspora during the last decade give up the 'American Dream' and pin its hopes on Spain? The ever increasing risk, harsher migratory policies, and the high cost of the trip to the United States made Spain and other European nations a safer and less expensive option.

With a backdrop of several years of economic and political instability, Ecuador reached a state of crisis in early 2000, when the Ecuadorian *sucre* was devalued 66% and the US dollar was adopted as the new national currency. According to the *Dirección Nacional de Migración* in Ecuador, between 1996 and July 2003, the number of Ecuadorians who left the country and did not return reached a total of 780,480 people (Sánchez, 2004, p. 50). This official number, however, does not reflect the thousands of people who have emigrated crossing borders illegally. The most recent literature on the subject affirms that approximately one million Ecuadorians migrated between 2000 and 2005 (Acosta, López, & Villamar, 2005, p. 228), and the most conservative calculations signal that 1.5 million Ecuadorians are currently living abroad, which represents more than 10% of Ecuador's total population, calculated at about 13 million people (Dávila, interview in *Just a Click Away from Home*).

As a consequence of the migratory stream at the turn of the century, Ecuador – whose economy has been historically centered on the exports of primary goods like coffee, cacao, bananas and, lately, petroleum – is now a country that exports its work force and has become heavily dependent on the income produced abroad by its diaspora.

Thus, electronic remittances to Ecuador increased from about 200 million US dollars in 1994 to 1.32 billion in 2000, becoming since then the second largest source of income for the country after oil exports (Acosta et al., 2005, p. 230). In 2004, according to the *Banco Central del Ecuador*, the country received 1.6 billion US dollars through remittances, whereas oil exports produced about 4.5 billion US dollars.[4]

Today, approximately one million of the 13 million residents living in Ecuador receive remittances. They get an average of 175 US dollars per wire transfer and about eight deliveries per year (Sánchez, 2004, p. 54). Apart from being more reliable than oil exports, remittances do not pass through State institutions, and go 'directly into people's pockets' (Dávila, interview in *Just a Click Away from Home*). In the midst of the economic collapse of 1999–2000 and the inflation generated by the devaluation of the *sucre*, as well as the adoption of the US dollar as the national currency, remittances became the saving grace that spared the country a complete collapse. On the one hand, the State was able to mask the lack of social investment that, always insufficient, fell to a lamentable proportion of total spending during and immediately after the crisis. On the other hand, those lucky enough to have relatives settled abroad managed to cover with remittances the loss of savings, the sudden reduction of their salaries, the unemployment, and the increase in the cost of living.

For many, then, remittances have provided the option to overcome unemployment or low salaries through small scale private initiatives: Internet based business ventures are a quintessential example of these initiatives. The acquisition of personal computers and related technology is still a luxury that only a few Ecuadorians can afford. The proliferation of cyber-cafés and *telecentros* throughout the national territory and in those places where the Ecuadorian diaspora has settled clearly illustrates how, in the case of Ecuador – as in those of many other Third World countries forced to export their human capital – mass migration and access to new technologies of information and communication intertwine in a symbiotic relation, generating a transnational strategy of survival.

Among the many negative consequences that the migratory phenomenon provoked in Ecuador, the multiplication of families torn up by migration is one of the most serious. Single-parent households and children living with their grandparents are frequently analysed as a phenomena intricately related to the emergence of violent teen gangs, for instance. Non-profit initiatives like the *Programa*

Migración, Comunicación y Desarrollo[5] try to confront the problem supporting the creation of *telecentros* to serve groups with high rates of migration and seriously deprived of access to new technologies. By June 2005 there were seven *telecentros* functioning in Ecuador. Far more numerous, however, are the cyber-cafés opened across the country by entrepreneurs. Thus, until 2004, there were 1,180 cyber-cafés registered in Ecuador: 84.57% of them appeared between 2000 and 2004, whereas only 15.43% had been registered before 2000 (Ramírez & Ramírez, 2005, pp. 95–96). Called *locutorios* in Spain and *phonecenters* in Italy, these businesses have become popular in those countries too, and they are often owned by migrants.

Ecuadorian researchers studying migration patterns warn of the possibility of a new economic collapse. They fear that the stream of remittances will soon begin to diminish due to processes of family reunification and permanent settlement in the host countries. Currently, financial institutions widely benefit from remittances with expensive charges for money transfer services: according to the Inter-American Development Bank (IDB), remittance fees average about 8% of the amount transferred (Ransom, 2006, para. 5).[6] However, local industries are not recovering from the crisis because a substantial portion of the remittances is sent abroad again through a mass consumption of imported goods. Meanwhile, those Ecuadorian communities that keep sending their youngest and, lately, quite qualified people to work as cheap laborers in the First World, do not experience major signs of development (Acosta et al., 2005, p. 250; Sánchez, 2004, p. 57). Paradoxically, those very same communities (the southern provinces of Azuay and Cañar in particular), where manual labor has become scarce and expensive, experience today the growing arrival of Colombian refugees and Peruvian temporary laborers. They come attracted to the higher wages and the payment in dollars. They call Ecuador 'the little US'.

Nostalgia, from modernity to postmodernity

Have new technologies transformed the experience of displacement for Ecuadorian migrants? How do they use them to cope with distance and nostalgia? Are they constructing transnational lives, families, and organizations through the recurring use of these technologies? In order to answer these questions, in June 2005 I began the production of the documentary video *Just a Click Away from Home*, which tells three different stories of migration from Ecuador to the United States, Spain and Italy, countries that have become the three main destinations for Ecuadorian immigrants during the past decade.

The documentary starts out with Mercedes and Arturo in Cuenca (Ecuador). They are experiencing the first videoconference of their lives. It is Father's Day and their five children living in New York City have decided to surprise them with a virtual encounter after 11 years of separation. Since they are undocumented immigrants, these children cannot leave the US to visit their relatives. Thus, videoconferencing technology becomes a replacement for face-to-face contact precluded by illegal migration. The second narration focuses on Gloria, whose husband, Luis, had migrated to Madrid five years earlier. Left in Ecuador, Gloria, and 30 other people founded the *Association of Migrants' Relatives Rumiñahui*. When they realized that access to new technologies could strengthen the communication with their relatives abroad, and thus save families torn apart by migration, they created *Ruminet*, a *telecentro* located in downtown Quito, where members and non-members obtain affordable access to Internet, as well as free instruction on basic computer operation. Finally, the documentary narrates the story of Carla, an Ecuadorian correspondent based in Milan who writes for *El Comercio*, the second largest national newspaper in Ecuador. While Carla uses digital photos, email, chat, and the Internet to report regularly on the successes and misfortunes of her compatriots settled in Italy, some immigrants choose to tell their stories by themselves: they take advantage of the same technologies to send images and texts to *Ecuadorians in the World*, a recently created section of *elcomercio.com*.

For this exploration of nostalgia I would like to focus on the first story and the very first sequence of the documentary, which shows Arturo, Mercedes and other relatives interacting through the videoconferencing screen with their kids settled in Queens, NY. 'Here and there, together, looking and talking. We were there together', says Vaneza, who had recently married the youngest of Mercedes and Arturo's children, Adrián. Interviewed in Queens after that first videoconference, Vaneza struggles to find the word that would better explain the situation: that word is simultaneity, and simultaneity is precisely one of the defining features of what I call digital nostalgia.

My conception of nostalgia, for the purposes of this essay, draws largely on the work of Svetlana Boym (2001, p. xiii), who argues that 'nostalgia (from *nostos*-return home, and *algia*-longing) is a longing for a home that no longer exists or has never existed. Nostalgia', she continues, 'is a sentiment of loss and displacement, but it is also a romance with one's own fantasy'. According to James Phillips (1985, p. 65), 'nostalgia is more subjective, less literal than homesickness', and it gives to terms such as exile and return a metaphoric meaning. Thus, in terms of nostalgia, home means a place as much as a time left behind. However, as Phillips puts it, the emphasis in modern nostalgia may have switched from space to time: 'Odysseus longs for home; Proust is in search of lost time. Further, since space is retraversable but time is not, the return is possible for the homesick exile in a way that is not for the nostalgic'. Yet, though time may be the privileged axis, the question of space should not be considered completely out of the picture in contemporary nostalgia. For one thing, attention to space reveals some of the power relations of global capitalism. As we see in the stories of Ecuadorian migration, while space may look more retraversable than ever for some (especially, perhaps, for insatiable First World tourists), it is plainly not retraversable for Mercedes and Arturo – who have been denied a visa to travel to the United States – or for their children, who are stuck in New York City, unable to temporarily leave the US due to their status as undocumented immigrants.

Originally coined by the Swiss physician Johannes Hofer, who in 1688 defended his thesis on nostalgia, the word designated a 'new disease' whose victims became obsessed with longing for their native land. Sailors and soldiers fighting abroad, as well as country people working in the cities were among the first diagnosed with nostalgia, and all shared the condition of having been forced to leave home (Starobinski, 1966, p. 84). As Boym (2001, p. 4) writes:

> Nostalgia operated by an 'associationist magic', by means of which all aspects of everyday life related to one single obsession … The nostalgic had an amazing capacity for remembering sensations, tastes, sounds, smells, the minutiae and trivia of the lost paradise that those who remained home never noticed.

The disease seemed under control during the years that followed Hofer's 'discovery' of nostalgia. 'Leeches, warm hypnotic emulsions, opium and a return to the Alps usually soothed the symptoms' of the nostalgic Swiss soldiers, and by the end of the seventeenth century nostalgia was seen as a curable, democratic ('unlike melancholia, which was regarded as an ailment of monks and philosophers') and even 'patriotic' disease, since it 'expressed love for freedom and one's native land' (Boym, 2001, p. 6). However, in his historic account of the birth of nostalgia, Jean Starobinski (1966, p. 86) affirms that by the end of the eighteenth century people started to avoid long stays away from home, fearful of the illness, since some 'even died of nostalgia after having read in books that nostalgia is a disease which is frequently mortal'.

When nostalgia was first diagnosed in the United States, during the Civil War, the American military doctor Theodore Calhoun conceived it as 'a shameful disease that revealed a lack of manliness and unprogressive attitudes' (Boym, 2001, p. 6). In the United States, nostalgia was seen as a disease directly related to 'a slow and inefficient use of time conducive to daydreaming, erotomania and onanism', as well as to a rural background:

> 'The soldier from the city cares not where he is or where he eats, while his country cousin pines for the old homestead and his father's groaning board', wrote Calhoun. In such cases, the only hope was that the advent of progress would somehow alleviate nostalgia and the efficient use of time would eliminate idleness, melancholy, procrastination and lovesickness. (Boym, 2001, p. 6)

The advent of progress, however, did nothing but to turn nostalgia into an incurable disease. By the end of the eighteenth century, the physicians started to report that the symptoms of nostalgia did not disappear anymore with the return home, and the epidemic began to spread with the same accelerated pace that modernization would take hold on daily life with its machines, railroads, and timetables. It is in this condition of incurability that nostalgia reaches our postindustrial times, and if I have focused on Boym's approach to the topic it is because her quest leads us to establish a direct link between nostalgia and the modern condition: 'How did it happen that a provincial ailment, *maladie du pays*, became a disease of the modern age, *mal du siècle*?' asks the author, and answers: 'the spread of nostalgia had to do not only with dislocation in space but also with the changing conception of time' (2001, p. 7).

It would appear then that Calhoun's cure for nostalgia – more efficient use of time and less daydreaming – was a direct cause of the disease. By the end of the nineteenth century, trains and railways, as well as the steam powered ships, had shortened the distances within the metropolis and between them and their colonies; moreover, electricity had been discovered and even the telegraph, the 'first binary medium of communication', was already at work (Petzold, 1999, p. 43). Quoting Leo Marx, Michael Adas (1989, p. 222) remarks that 'the railroad system incorporated most of the essential features of the emerging industrial order', among them 'speed, rationality, impersonality, and an unprecedented emphasis on precise timing'.

On one hand, these technological developments made it easier for displaced people to visit home (although they also facilitated displacements to remote destinations, where frequently people would build a new home and never come back to their native land). On the other hand, the capitalist system had not invested in technology just to take care of nostalgic souls: the new machines were basically used to accelerate revenues through automated and quicker processes of production.

In the cities, workers were integrated to the pace of the restless machines, becoming cyborgs with no time to visit their native village or to even think about it.

> Punctuality was at a premium; tardiness was 'paid for' by fines or loss of employment; and machines set the pace at which men, women, and children labored. Time became a commodity that could be 'saved', 'spent', or 'wasted'. Laborers sold it; entrepreneurs bought it. (Adas, 1989, p. 242)

The same way that, in the United States, Doctor Calhoun criticized the slow and inefficient use of time by nostalgic rural soldiers, in the early nineteenth century those Europeans that colonized Africa and Asia could not see the cultures they encountered but through the lens of their societies 'dominated by clocks, railway schedules, and mechanical rhythms'. According to Adas (1989, p. 243), 'they "went out" to cultures still closely attuned to the cycles of nature, to societies in which leisure was savored, patience was highly regarded, and everyday life moved at a pace that most Western intruders found enervating if not downright exasperating'. From then on, as it happened with nostalgia, those paces of everyday life that do not conform to the Western model of time-commodity have been identified with backwardness and unprogressive attitudes.

Nostalgia was born, then, inscribed in the nature of the modern age, and should be understood not only as the longing for a lost home, but also for a time when time was not necessarily conceived as money. This incurable disease of longing must have spread even more in our late capitalist age, initiated in the developed world during the second half of the twentieth century, and characterized by an extraordinary time-space compression process made possible by the conjunction of communication and digital technologies.

A matter of speed

Boym (2001, p.10) borrows from Reinhart Koselleck two categories that can help us to understand the shift in the conception of time during the modern age: 'space of experience' and 'horizon of expectation'. 'The space of experience allows one to account for the assimilation of the past into the present', whereas the 'horizon of expectation reveals the way of thinking about the future'. According to Koselleck, what definitely changed the conception of time was the introduction of the idea of progress:

> The idea of progress, once it moved from the realm of arts and sciences to the ideology of industrial capitalism, became a new theology of 'objective' time. Progress is the first genuinely historical concept which reduced the temporal difference between experience and expectation to a single concept. (as cited in Boym, 2001, p. 10)

If at the beginning of the modern era philosophers like Kant played with the idea of time as a subjective experience, the teleology of progress imposed an objective time, measurable to the detail (railroad timetables) and characterized by a 'shrinking space of experience that no longer fits the new horizon of expectations' (2001, p.10).

Once time had been 'objectivized', efficiency in its use became a matter of speed, as Calhoun made clear in the nineteenth century, when he found nostalgia was a product of 'inefficient' and 'slow' use of time. Calhoun's diagnosis of nostalgia could actually be interpreted as an early manifestation of what Scott Bukatman (2003, p. 41) calls the 'perpetual, agitated kinesis' of the American spirit, a spirit for which 'the body is a machine, perfectible and progress oriented, while – at the same time – the machine becomes a body'. Bukatman illustrates his assertion with an anecdote:

> The symbiosis of typewriter (machine) and typewriter (user) probably reached an apotheosis around the speed-typing exhibitions that swept the country for about thirty-five years beginning in the late 1800s ... Before the battles, typewriter manufacturers had been content to boast that typing was twice as fast as the hand, but now these typewriter cyborgs, these paper cowboys, left the natural hand far behind on the evolutionary ladder. One charming and slightly scary photo shows the 1926 amateur (!) champion, Stella Willins, posing in a motorcycle sidecar with her typewriter (of course) perched precariously before her. It's as though her typing must be measured in mph instead of wpm. (2003, p. 41)

Thus, almost a century ago, typewriters' battles were already advertising speed as a result of a new technology, practically the same way that TV ads sell us today a faster computer or a quicker connection to the Internet. The postmodern quest for efficiency, however, goes beyond speed and acceleration: the technological race of today – still lead by the United States – will not accept less than 'instantaneity' (Bell, 2001, p. 86).

Transposed to the realm of daily life, this quest for instantaneity has not meant more time available, but rather the opposite: a continuous shrinking of time. The counting of keystrokes per minute became a popular measure of efficiency in the golden years of typewriters, and the practice continues today, only now computers do the counting and are entrusted to measure how efficient their users are. Thus every minute counts in this late capitalist age, when tasks can be finished much more quickly, but one is expected to complete many more tasks than before, and to complete them all at the same time, simultaneously. It is because we live under this 'perpetual time pressure' that, as Svetlana Boym (2001, p. 351) affirms, 'contemporary nostalgia is not so much about the past as about the vanishing present'.

If the present vanishes in the expectations of the future, without giving us the chance to digest it, what we are missing is the experience of continuity, the cement that holds together the isolated events transforming them in episodes in the narratives of memory or history. Thus nostalgia in our times is also a longing for that continuity of events that now, thanks to the ever improving speed of technology, is becoming simultaneity. Lots of data, lots of tasks, lots of events happen at the same time, while we struggle against time to establish connections and to make some sense of them.

Analog human beings vs digital technologies

In the nineteenth century people had to adjust to the pace of the analog machines and learn how to deal with the timetables in train stations. Today, we struggle to keep up with the breathtaking rhythm of digital machines that most of us do not even understand. According to Charles Petzold (1999, p. 365), 'people and computers are very different animals, and unfortunately it's easier to persuade people to make adjustments to accommodate the peculiarities of computers than the other way around'. Steam powered trains or ships were analog machines, whose operation simulated processes that people had seen before in nature and in the functioning of their own bodies. Although in a fairly general way, this 'analogy' helps us understand how these and other analog machines work. Moreover, their activity crosses time and space in a visible way that allows us grasp the link between a movement and its effect, the process, the continuity.

On the other hand, just a few initiated understand what is going on inside those magical boxes called computers, which are apparently able to transform any kind of information to a binary code of zeros and ones. As Petzold says, computers are quite different animals from us: even when the box is open, we cannot see the continuity of movements crossing space and time to produce an effect. Digital machines do not operate physically like something we could recognize in nature and, above all, they do not 'think' of time or space the way human beings do:

> The machine seemed to understand time and space, but it didn't, not as we do. We are analog, fluid, swimming in a flowing sea of events, where one moment contains the next, *is* the next, since the notion of 'moment' itself is the illusion. The machine – it – is digital, and digital is the decision to forget the idea of the infinitely moving wave, and just take snapshots, convincing yourself that if you take enough pictures, it won't matter that you've left out the flowing, continuous aspect of things. You take the mimic for the thing mimicked and say, Good enough. But now I knew that between one pixel and the next – no matter how densely together you packed them – the world still existed, down to the finest grain of the stuff of the universe. (Ullman, 2003, pp. 347–48)

This passage comes from Ellen Ullman's novel *The Bug,* whose main subject is precisely the struggle to reconcile analog human beings with digital machines. Not by chance, Ullman situates her story in the mid-1980s, when the quest for narrowing the gap between analog human beings and digital machines had lead software developers to the invention of the *graphical user interface* (GUI). The user interface is 'the point at which human and computer meet' (Petzold, 1999, p. 365). In the beginnings of the computer age, this point used to be a punched card, where the programmer put instructions and received answers from the computer. Later the cards evolved into rolls of paper where a teletype would write text in computer language. When the first monitors appeared, they were still used as if the screen were a roll of paper scrolling up and down. This interface was still being used in the early 1980s, when the PCs started to 'democratize' the access to computers.

Already in the late 1960s, scientists from the Palo Alto Research Center (PARC) had developed the Alto, a computer that could interact with its users through a computer graphic interface, which means basically the transformation of the screen in a space where digital graphics represent familiar objects from physical reality (a desktop, a file, a paper sheet), in order to make easier the communication between the computer and its user. The Alto, however, was too expensive, and the idea would not become a successful product until a decade later.[7]

Nowadays, Windows is the most used operating system with a computer graphic interface. With the help of the mouse, which is usually represented on the screen as a moving pointer, the graphic interface tries to erase the gap between analog human being and digital machine giving the user the impression of continuity of space and time. Lots of digital objects populate the screen, and we have the illusion of moving through space and time in order to reach a specific object and 'open' it. Sometimes, while we wait for the computer to accomplish an order, time passing is represented on screen by a sandglass, a graphic-nostalgic relic from the good old times when time had not been strictly measured in order to ensure efficiency.

Instantaneity has not been accomplished yet, and computers fake that they can understand how the passing of time feels, but they don't. The 'flowing sea of events' that Ullman describes in her novel is what we, analog creatures, have come to conceive of as time. Thus time for us is about the connection of one instant with the previous and the next one, about that continuity between them that Bergson (1999, p. 30) calls duration: 'a memory that prolongs the before into the after, keeping them from being mere snapshots and appearing and disappearing in a present ceaselessly reborn'. Digital machines, on the other hand, inhabit that present ceaselessly reborn. There, digital objects are created anew every time we open their files.

Digital nostalgia

To propose that nostalgia might be becoming digital, then, is to propose an oxymoron. Whereas digital implies a permanent present inhabited by all the snapshots and all their possible arrangements at the same time, nostalgia is about understanding time as a fluid stream that turns into irrecoverable past all that it touches. This oxymoron, however, may be useful to explain how displacement and uprooting feel in the age of globalization, in a world of global-local tensions, where reinforced borders coexist with fluid subjects and identities.

If nostalgia had appeared in the seventeenth century as a disease that affected people physically displaced from their native land, it spread during the modern age as an epidemic worsened by the objectivization of space that accompanied the objectivization of time. After all, 'progress was not only a narrative of temporal progression but also of spatial expansion' (Boym, 2001, p. 10). There had been a time when distances were relatively short – most people used not to venture too far from home – and were measured with parts of the body (whose length, obviously, changed according to the size of the body in question). In the modern era, however, the process of objectivization of space that had started with the development of perspective during the Renaissance became the rule. Progress meant the multi-plication of possibilities to travel and colonize remote places far from the metropolis, and such a territorial expansion required 'mapping the new discovered worlds'. In order to rationalize the collection of taxes and to ensure its political control over a number of local realities 'impenetrable and misleading to outsiders', a 'common denominator, a common map', was imposed by the logic of progress. 'Thus modernization meant making the populated world hospitable to supracommunal, state-ruled administration bureaucracy and moving from a bewildering diversity of maps to a universally shared world' (Boym, 2001, p. 11). In that new universalized, measured, objectivized space, those who remained at home may have been as prone to nostalgia as those who traveled to remote destinations, because they were also being displaced from their world as they knew it.

In the late capitalist age, however, that objectivized space seems to disappear under our feet in the midst of the process of globalization. As Stuart Hall affirms, globalization is an old process whose origins could be traced at least back to the formation of the modern nation-states and the colonial empires. However, what is currently named as globalization refers generally to some of the new 'forms, rhythms and impetuses' of the globalizing process (Hall, 1997, p. 20). Global commodities and financial markets, new digital technologies, 'which have linked production and markets in a new surge of international global capital', and a new multinational production which 'links backward sections of the third world to so-called advanced sections of the first world' constitute, according to Hall, an old way to think about globalization which has been broken up by the 'enormous, continuing migrations of labor in the post-war world'.

> There is a tremendous paradox here which I cannot help relishing myself; that in the very moment when finally Britain convinced itself it had to decolonize, it had to get rid of them, we all came back home. As they hauled down the flag, we got on the banana boat and sailed right into London. (Hall, 1997, p. 24)

The paradox not only applies to England, but also to other colonialist metropolises such as Paris and Madrid, as well as to the neocolonialism of the United States, whose first grand demonstration of power was the victory in the American-Spanish-Cuban-Phillippino war (1898), that snatched Cuba, Puerto Rico and Philippines from Spanish rule and helped to define Latin America as the 'backyard' of the United States. In the same way that Hall left Jamaica to settle in Britain, 1.5 million Ecuadorians have recently moved to the United States, Spain or Italy, whereas millions of Africans, Asians, South Asians, Latin Americans and Caribbean people continue to move towards the First World today, in a continued flux that, according to Arjun Appadurai (1996, p. 41), marks another paradox within the globalization process:

> The central paradox of ethnic politics in today's world is that primordia (whether of language or skin color or neighborhood or kinship) have become globalized. That is, sentiments, whose greatest force is in their ability to ignite intimacy into a political state and turn locality into a staging ground for identity, have become spread over vast and irregular spaces as groups move yet stay linked to one another through sophisticated media capabilities ... Because of the disjunctive and unstable interplay of commerce, media, national policies, and consumer fantasies, ethnicity, once a genie contained in the bottle of some sort of locality (however large), has now become a global force, forever slipping in and through the cracks between states and borders.

*Ethnoscape*s is how Appadurai (1996, pp. 33–34) labels this paradox, where the landscapes of relatively stable communities and networks of kinship, friendship or work constitute a warp 'everywhere shot through with the woof of human motion, as more persons and groups deal with the realities of having to move or the fantasies of wanting to move'. It is within these *ethnoscapes*, understood as a core element of the current process of globalization, that digital nostalgia may be found, as one of those sentiments that, as Appadurai would put it, have become spread over vast and irregular spaces created by sophisticated media capabilities, and slip through the cracks between states and borders. It is within the contradictory discourses of globalization, which relentlessly sell an emergent 'global culture' and the erasure of space, distance and borders, while encouraging legal and territorial barriers (e.g. the United States/Mexico borderline) that prevent the free circulation of people between developed and underdeveloped worlds, that digital nostalgia should be located and understood.

Let's go back then to the videoconference sequence in *Just a Click Away from Home* and see digital nostalgia at work. Mercedes and Arturo have been brought to the videoconferencing center by three of their eight children to see, for the first time in several years, their other five kids, who emigrated to the United States and currently live in Queens. Paúl and Armando, the two older brothers, arrived in the United States 11 years earlier, whereas the other three (William, Juan and Adrián) have been living in New York for the previous five years. Since none of them has yet been able to obtain a legal immigrant status, they cannot leave the US to visit their relatives in Ecuador or to check the progress of the real estate investments they maintain in their home country.[8] The videoconference is the ultimate technological medium they have used in order to deal with distance and nostalgia. It is inscribed, however, in a long chain of other resources – many of them designed to profit on the nostalgic market of immigrants – that allow them to live with one foot in Queens, and the other in Cuenca. Among these resources is electronic mail (Juan and William maintain regular contact with their siblings in Ecuador through email), the World Wide Web (Adrián keeps posted on investment opportunities published by Ecuadorian real estate companies on web sites), the electronic remittances that they send to their parents in a monthly basis, the inexpensive phone cards that they use to call to Ecuador every week and, of course, the delicatessen of traditional Ecuadorian dishes that their parents send on special occasions (such as birthdays) through quick delivery service companies.

Whereas Vaneza is struck by the experience of simultaneity that the videoconference produces, her husband, Adrián, reflects on how being able to see his parents – in real time and almost real size – reinforced his desire/impression of continuity with them:

> Maybe, that's the next best thing. To be able to see them, at least, on a big screen, and to have direct communication with them. It's not like the phone, you know? With the phone you can only hear and the rest is left up to the imagination: what are they doing? Where are they? Who are they with?

Digital nostalgia, as it seems to be experienced by Vaneza and Adrián, is the quest for continuity of space and time through the simultaneity offered by digital media. In a way, digital nostalgia may mean basically the disappearance of nostalgia as we knew it. As we have seen, nostalgia was born and became an incurable disease during the modern age, when the idea of progress shrank the temporal difference between experience and expectation into a concept that contained both, a concept that made experience (the past) and expectation (the future) one and equivalent. Transposed to the realm of daily life, progress meant that time had become objective, measurable, a valuable commodity. Thus progress meant also the multiplication of nostalgic souls who longed for those days when it was still possible to taste time in your own subjective way, when patience and leisure were values and no one had heard about time efficient procedures. Late capitalism, on the other hand, is taking the time-space compression process initiated in the industrial era to the digital extreme. It is not about progress anymore, since past and future never meet in the permanent and multiple presents that cohabit simultaneously in our everyday life, where now we are not only expected to efficiently complete a task at a time, but to multitask efficiently. If nostalgia as we knew it was all about idealization and one's own romance with the time and the home left behind (Boym, 2001, p. xiii), digital nostalgia is about the annihilation of longing through constant and real-time exposure to a home and a time that are never really left behind, since digital technologies today allow us to virtually be in many places at the same time.

As Adrián explains when interviewed in *Just a Click Away from Home*, with the videoconference there is not much material left for the imagination. In the particular case of immigrants, for instance, new technologies seem to be narrowing the space of longing for an idealized home. Gloria Orellana, the owner of *Ecuadorian*

Phonecenter in Milan, whom I interviewed for the documentary, affirms that for many of her customers, being able to call home frequently does not seem to help them heal nostalgia:

> It's always the family: 'I told you to do this and you haven't done it. This one's in a bad situation ... The other is sick ... ' They leave the *phonecenter* desperate, crying. 'I have to send money', they say. 'From home they are always asking for money'.

Apparently, migrant workers' lives have become a daily negotiation between the challenges presented by the reality they physically inhabit and those other commitments based in their home countries, where their families, and ultimately the whole country, depend significantly on their decisions ... and their remittances.

The virtual erasure of the distance, the impression of continuity created by digital technologies may be turning nostalgia in a sentiment 'less acute but much more present', says Alberto Acosta, one of the experts in Ecuadorian migration interviewed in the documentary. 'In some senses, it can be quite painful', he adds. 'In the past, when there was a family breakup, for instance, this rupture may not have seemed that serious for the person living abroad, because of the distance: "out of sight, out of mind", the saying goes'. Conversely, today 'one might be more connected with the family and it can be more difficult to heal that wound and move on'.

In terms of the shrinking of space, digital nostalgia seems to rely strongly on the visuals to strengthen the impression of proximity and continuity. From the interviews with Ecuadorian immigrants in *Just a Click Away from Home*, it is clear that the more they can see of that home left behind, the more they are unable to keep it out of sight, the more attached they become to that home ever present in their minds. The sight, however, may not be as beautiful as those idealized memories of family, home, and country that migrants and exiles would nurture three decades ago. Back then, new technologies had not shrunk space that much yet; therefore, the distance and/or the impossibility of return would only contribute to make that home left behind look like a lost paradise in displaced people's memories.

Sitting in his living room in Queens with a laptop, Adrián – the youngest of Arturo and Mercedes' children living in the US – takes advantage of whatever free time he gets to check out real estate business possibilities on the Internet. When I ask him if he is looking for some property in New York, he quickly replies 'no, in Cuenca'. 'As I told you before', he explains, 'I want to go back to Ecuador. So, I like to check out what properties are available and things like that'. This particular day, Adrián has found a medium sized house near the stadium and we both look at the photos on the screen. 'It's too expensive', he says, 'it costs 275,000 dollars'. The high levels of speculation provoked in Cuenca by the dollarization and the migratory phenomenon may be news for his interviewer, but not for Adrián, who follows this ritual almost every day and keeps himself up to date on what is going on with the real estate market in his city. Without a gram of surprise, he turns away from the laptop and says with some irony: 'I would have to stay here 20 more years to buy that house!' In a way, this digital quest for a good investment and a safe return to Ecuador might be part of what keeps Adrián from going back home: life in Cuenca, he knows, could be even harder now than it used to be when he left, in 2000.

Digital nostalgia, however, goes beyond the annihilation of longing and not necessarily towards a dead end. Today, some digital nostalgic migrants may be said to take advantage of digital technologies to follow the 'pulse' of their countries in some cases more closely than many of those who remained at home. Theirs tends to be a much less embellished and rather critical image of the home left behind. While the simultaneity offered by digital technologies allows them to find out what is going on in their home countries almost at the same time that the events are happening, the effect of continuity that this simultaneity produces seems to nourish a desire to participate, to belong, to be part of those processes that will define the destiny of a country that they never completely left behind.

A clear sign of the connection between access to new technologies and this growing desire to secure a sense of belonging is the appearance of grass-roots migrant organizations that not only use the *telecentro*, the *locutorio*, or the *phonecenter* as their headquarters, but are also a product of the existence of such places where digital technology can be used to erase distance. The first time I visited Ecuadorian Phonecenter in Milan, for instance, I had planned to have an interview with the owner, Gloria Orellana, but ended up attending a meeting of the Federation of Ecuadorian Immigrants, Milan branch. 'I have this business where so many Ecuadorians come. Maybe we can put something together', Gloria says in the documentary *Just a Click Away from Home*, remembering how the idea of forming the Federation was born. 'We are now registering Ecuadorians in the area to vote. They can come here to the *phonecenter* and register', Gloria adds later on. From Italy, Spain, the US, and many other settlement countries, the Ecuadorian diaspora used the growing importance of remittances for the country's economy to argue in favor of their right to vote. Thus, a new law was approved and, in 2006, Ecuadorian migrants settled all over the world cast in embassies and consulates their votes for the new President of the Republic.

So, in one instantiation, digital nostalgia is about the annihilation of longing, as we see in the case of migrant workers who are followed by the complications and needs from home wherever they can be reached by email or phone. Here, overexposure to home leaves no time or space for longing. Yet, digital nostalgia is also about the conscious use of the simultaneity offered by digital technologies to construct an 'effect' of continuity: all those displaced people who have been increasingly getting involved in their country's current affairs through the use of web sites, blogs, email or other digital tools are deliberately using the effect of continuity – the erasure of distance – to strengthen a sense of belonging. This strategic move might be helping them reverse the global process of fragmentation and uprooting of individuals in postmodern societies.

Acknowledgements

A very special thank you to Regina Harrison, my dissertation advisor, who generously guided me through the obscure first steps of this work. I also would like to thank Susan Antebi, Alessandro Fornazzari, and particularly Freya Schywi, for their enormous effort in putting together this special issue of *Social Identities*. I want to thank, as well, our anonymous reader, whose pertinent suggestions I have tried to incorporate in this last version of the essay. And finally, I would like to express my deepest gratitude to my husband, David Morrow, who has patiently reviewed innumerable versions of this text and encouraged me to enrich it and keep working on it ... even though that always meant more work for him too.

Notes

1. As explained by Matías Zibell in the article 'El sombrero que no era de Panamá', the *toquilla* straw grows in the coastal province of Manabí. Here is located the town of Montecristi, where the world's finest 'Panama hats' are woven. In Montecristi, a few masters take months to weave a hat that costs about 500 US dollars. However, the center of mass production of these hats is located in southern Ecuador. The *toquilla* straw is delivered from Manabí to thousands of weavers spread in the provinces of Azuay and Cañar. They will take a few days to produce a hat valued at about 8 to 10 US dollars. Historically, Cuenca, capital of the province of Azuay, has been the center of straw hat exports.

2. The Latin American Debt Crisis exploded in 1982, when Mexico announced that it was unable to service the debt to international creditors. Like Mexico, Ecuador had acquired many short-term credits throughout the 1970s for industrialization and infrastructure programs. Also, during the 1970s, vast oil reserves were discovered in Ecuadorian territory, and oil exports became the main source of income for the country. However, in the early 1980s, when oil prices dropped and international creditors raised interest rates, Mexico collapsed and the rest of Latin American nations collapsed along with it. Those governments that had been hoping to renegotiate their short-term loans found that creditors would not lend to them anymore. As private capital fled Ecuador, the national currency was devalued and, as in the case of most countries in the region, Ecuador adopted the neo-liberal structural adjustment programs designed by the International Monetary Fund (IMF).

3. According to the press in Ecuador, between 750,000 and 1,000,000 Ecuadorians live currently in the United States. These numbers practically double the information obtained by the US Census Bureau, which in 2000 determined that 396,400 people of Ecuadorian descent live in the US territory, most of them – 177,957 – in New York City, concentrated principally in the borough of Queens. Between 1990 and 2000, the Ecuadorian population in the United States grew 53.7%, according to the Census Bureau. The percentage could be even greater if one takes into account that the majority of Ecuadorian immigrants get to the United States illegally and, in consequence, tend to avoid being counted in the census (Jokisch, 2001, para 2). In Spain, according to data released by the *Instituto Nacional de Estadísticas*, in 2004 there were about 390,000 Ecuadorians. Thus the Ecuadorian community became the most numerous (Troya, 2005, p. 154). As for Italy, it has been estimated that approximately 100,000 Ecuadorian immigrants live currently there, with a 50% of them concentrated in the cities of Milan and Turin (Avilés, 2005, p. 133).

4. The difference between the two incomes in this particular year may seem enormous but, put in context, it actually reflects one of the main advantages of remittances: their steady growth and reliability, as opposed to the unstable behavior of oil export prices, governed by the capricious global market. In 1998, for instance, due to the falling prices of petroleum, oil exports and remittances provided the country with almost exactly the same income: about one billion US dollars each. Whereas since 2001 the Ecuadorian diaspora has steadily sent to the country approximately 1.5 billion US dollars per year, oil exports have followed an erratic pattern that varies from about 2.5 billion US dollars in the year 2000 to 2 billion in 2001 as well as the already mentioned 4.8 billion in 2004, a direct consequence of the war in Iraq and the rise in the prices of petroleum provoked by the conflict (Acosta et al., 2005, p. 232).

5. The Migration, Communication and Development Project partners non-profit organizations from Ecuador and Spain in a joint effort to coordinate initiatives related to the phenomenon of migration. Their main goal is to transform Ecuadorian migration into a generator of cultural exchange and co-development between Ecuador and Spain. The project started in 2001. In the documentary video *Just a Click Away from Home*, three leaders involved in the Project are interviewed: Alberto Acosta, Luis Dávila and Father Fernando Vega (head of the *Pastoral Social de Cuenca*).

6. According to Acosta et al. (2005, p. 250), 'in the case of the remittances sent from Spain, fees fluctuate between 3.7% and 14.4% of the total amount, while in the case of those sent from the United States it has been estimated that the transfer services charge between 10 and 30%'.

7. 'In 1979, Steve Jobs and a contingent from Apple Computer visited PARC and were quite impressed with what they saw. But it took them over three years to introduce a computer that had a graphical interface. This was the ill-fated Apple Lisa in January 1983. A year later, however, Apple introduced the much more successful Macintosh' (Petzold, 1999, p. 370).

8. In the United States, although the number of Ecuadorian immigrants has augmented rapidly during the past decade, they constitute the seventh group of Latin American descent population in the country: a minority within a minority (Hispanics for government and corporations and Latinos for grassroots movements). Whereas Puerto Ricans circulate freely between the island and New York in the 'guagua aérea' (aerial bus), and other Latin American immigrants like Salvadorans or Guatemalans have legalized their situation through amnesties, most Ecuadorians must interact with illegal transnationalism in order to enter the US, and there are no agreements between governments that could allow them to cross the threshold of illegality.

References

Acosta, A., López, S., & Villamar, D. (2005). Las remesas y su aporte para la economía ecuatoriana. In G. Herrera, M.C. Carrillo & A. Torres (Eds.), *La migración ecuatoriana: Transnacionalismo, redes e identidades* (pp. 227–52). Quito: Flacso-Plan Migración, Comunicación y Desarrollo.

Adas, M. (1989). *Machines as the measure of men. Science, technology, and ideologies of western dominance.* Ithaca: Cornell University Press.

Appadurai, A. (1996). *Modernity at large: Cultural dimensions of globalization.* Minneapolis: University of Minnesota Press.

Avilés, L.P. (2005). Reseña histórica sobre la emigración ecuatoriana a Italia: Situación actual y perspectivas. In J. Ponce Leiva (Ed.), *Emigración y política exterior en Ecuador* (pp. 123–46). Quito: Ediciones Abya-Yala.

Bell, D. (2001). *An introduction to cybercultures.* London: Routledge.

Bergson, H. (1999). *Duration and simultaneity.* R. Durie (Ed.). L. Jacobson (Trans.). Manchester: Clinamen Press.

Boym, S. (2001). *The future of nostalgia.* New York: Basic Books.

Bukatman, S. (2003). *Matters of gravity. Special effects and supermen in the 20th century.* Durham & London: Duke University Press.

Hall, S. (1997). The local and the global: Globalization and ethnicity. In A.D. King (Ed.), *Culture, globalization and the world system 1900–1940* (pp. 19–39). Minneapolis: University of Minnesota Press.

Herrera, G., Carrillo, M.C., & Torres, A. (Eds.). (2005). *La migración ecuatoriana: Transnacionalismo, redes e identidades.* Quito: FLACSO-Plan Migración, Comunicación y Desarrollo.

Jokisch, B. (2001). Desde Nueva York a Madrid: Tendencias en la migración ecuatoriana. *Ecuador Debate,* 54. Retrieved 24 October 2007 from www.dlh.lahora.com.ec/paginas/debate/paginas/debate313.htm

Kyle, D. (2000). *The transnational peasant: Migration networks and ethnicity in Andean Ecuador.* Baltimore: The Johns Hopkins University Press.

Mejía Estévez, S. (Producer & Director). (2007). *Just a click away from home.* [Documentary video]. United States. Available from Silvia Mejía Estévez, 432 Western Ave., The College of Saint Rose, Albany, NY 12203.

Petzold, C. (1999). *Code. The hidden language of computer hardware and software.* Redmond: Microsoft Press.

Phillips, J. (1985). Distance, absence, and nostalgia. In D. Ihde & H. J. Silverman (Eds.), *Descriptions* (pp. 64–75). Albany: State University of New York Press.

Ramírez, F., & Ramírez, J.P. (2005). Redes transnacionales y repertorios de acción migratoria: de Quito y Guayaquil para las ciudades del Primer Mundo. In G. Herrera, M.C. Carrillo & A. Torres (Eds.), *La migración ecuatoriana: Transnacionalismo, redes e identidades* (pp. 71–103). Quito: Flacso-Plan Migración, Comunicación y Desarrollo.

Ransom, D. (2006, January 26). Banks aim to help immigrants send money home. *The Christian Science Monitor*. Retrieved 22 March 2007 from http://www.csmonitor.com/2006/0126/p15s01-lifp.html

Sánchez, J. (2004). Ensayo sobre la economía de la emigración en Ecuador. *Ecuador Debate, 63*, 47–62.

Starobinski, J. (1966). The idea of nostalgia. *Diogenes, 54*, 81–103.

Troya, M.G. (2005). Ecuador y la política migratoria de la Unión Europea. In J. Ponce Leiva (Ed.), *Emigración y política exterior en Ecuador* (pp. 147–96). Quito: Ediciones Abya-Yala.

Ullman, E. (2003). *The bug: A novel*. New York: Doubleday.

Zibell, M. (2007, March 15). El sombrero que no era de Panamá. Part I. *Los blogs de BBC Mundo*. Retrieved 23 March 2007 from http://www.bbc.co.uk/blogs/spanish/2007/03/el_sombrero_que_no_era_de_pana.html

Zibell, M. (2007, March 20). El sombrero que no era de Panamá. Part II. *Los blogs de BBC Mundo*. Retrieved 23 March 2007 from http://www.bbc.co.uk/blogs/spanish/2007/03/el_sombrero_ii.html

Index

Alto 108
American Comparative Literature
  Association: meeting 2007 3
Antebi, Susan: talk shows, on 3
Autonomia perspective 1

Bigo, Didier: transnationalization of security
  networks, on 97
Biopower: nature of 29–30
Bolivia: digital technology, purpose of 25–26;
  distribution of videos 33; indigenous
  intercultural exchange 26–2; indigenous
  media 33; indigenous movements 23;
  individual responsibility of film makers 32–
  33; media activists 32; National Indigenous
  Plan for Audiovisual Communication 1996
  23; pre-colonial socio-economic relations
  34; *Qati Qati/ Whispers of Death* 31; *Qulqi
  Chaliku/Silver Vest* 31
Bony, Oscar 45
Border: meaning 95–96
Border economy 31–36
Boym, Svetlana: nostalgia, on 104
Bozzo, Laura: bloggers, and 7–8; *cholo* figure,
  and 14–15; construction of scenarios 13;
  critique of 7; hidden cameras 13;
  hypersaturated version 19–20; image of 11–
  12; Neo TV, and 13; Paleo TV, and 13;
  Pisco earthquake, and 12; racism, criticism
  of 14; violence on talkshow 12
Butler, Judith: maternity of body, on 10

Calhoun, Theodore: nostalgia, on 105–106
Cameraphones 59–80; accidental journalism
  64; age of digital reproduction as work of
  art 76–77; aura 68; authentication 68;
  catching a fish 59–60, 77; cherry blossom
  74–75; citizen journalism 64;
  commonplace, and 71; counter-tourism,
  and 71–72; cover of *New Yorker* 67;
  development of cell phone technology 60–
  61; digital image as tourist commodity 70;
  digital tourism 67–68; Donald Rumsfeld,

and 63; ephemerality 69; everyday, and 71;
flower viewing 74–75; format 62;
generation gaps 62–63; Great Buddha,
pictures of 72–73; hermeneutic circle 68;
historicity machine 69; Ian McEwan on 63;
instant nostalgia 69–70; insufficient "now"
75–76; Japan 59–60; keitai culture 64–65;
killing dead time 65–66; labor for
consumer 76; landscapes, pictures of 71;
London bombings 7 July 2005, and 63–64;
mass transit, and 66; Mizuko Ito, and 63;
mode of human sense perception, and 75;
Moore's law 60; narrativizing of images in
social context 74; object of the gaze 70;
origin 62; oxymoronics 61–62; pedestrian
narratives 73–74; people, pictures of 71;
perception 60; reframing of visual
discourses 66–67; scenery, pictures of 71;
speed 60; super-authenticity 68; talismania
72–73; tourism, and 71–72; tourist-*flâneur*-
photographer 69; tourist practices, and 61;
tribe of the thumb 65; usage patterns 61;
wasted hours, and 65–66; weapons of mass
photography 63
Castro-Gomez, Santiago: colonialism, and 28
Childers, Joseph
Chile: agrarian reform 84–85; *latifundio*
system 85; neoliberal reforms 85–86
Colonial legacies: capitalism, and 35
Copa, Alfredo: *Desempolvando* 33
Corporeality: digital media, and 9
Cullenberg, Stephen: unremarked labor, on 55
Cybernetics: humans as intelligent machines
24–25

Day-laboring: labor theory of value, and 54–
55
de Soto, Hernando: effect of capital, on 55
Devis, Juan 40–58; *245 (d) 1* 50–51; capital
implications 40–58; choice of format 41;
earlier work 40–41; function of labor in
video art 40–58; *Inter-State: Video on the
Go* 40, 41; Devis/Okon segment 42;

Routledge
Taylor & Francis Group

2008
Special Issue

Patterns of Prejudice

Special Issue - Volume 42, Number 4/5, October 2008
Naming Race, Naming Racisms
A special issue guest edited by **Jonathan Judaken**

Naming race, naming racisms: an introduction
Jonathan Judaken

Antinomies of race: diversity and destiny in Kant
Mark Larrimore

A Haitian in Paris: Anténor Firmin as a philosopher against racism
Robert Bernasconi

Surviving Maurras: Jacques Maritain's Jewish Question
Richard Francis Crane

Kenneth B. Clark and the problem of power
Damon Freeman

Listening to melancholia: Alice Walker's Meridian
Leigh Anne Duck

Riots, disasters and racism: impending racial cataclysm and the extreme right in the United States
George Michael and **D. J. Mulloy**

Assia Djebar's *qalam*: the poetics of the trace in postcolonial Algeria
Brigitte Weltman-Aron

'Everybody else just living their lives': 9/11, race and the new postglobal literature
Alfred J. Loepez

So what's new? Rethinking the 'new antisemitism' in a global age
Jonathan Judaken

Editors:
David Cesarani - *University of London, UK*
Tony Kushner and **Barbara Rosenbaum** - both at *University of Southampton, UK*

Volume 43, 2009, 5 issues per year
Print ISSN: 0031-322X, Online ISSN: 1461-7331

2007 Impact Factor: 0.302
Ranking: 5/9 (Ethnic Studies)
© Thomson Reuters Journal Citation Reports 2008

Patterns of Prejudice provides a forum for exploring the historical roots and contemporary varieties of social exclusion and the demonization or stigmatisation of the Other. It probes the language and construction of 'race', nation, colour, and ethnicity, as well as the linkages between these categories. It encourages discussion of issues at the top of the public policy agenda, such as asylum, immigration, hate crimes and citizenship. As none of these issues are confined to any one region, Patterns of Prejudice maintains a global optic, at the same time as scrutinizing intensely the history and development of intolerance and chauvinism in the United States and Europe, both East and West.

For further information, please contact Customer Services quoting promo code **XA 073 01 A** at either:

T&F Informa UK Ltd, Sheepen Place, Colchester, Essex, CO3 3LP, UK
Tel: +44 (0) 20 7017 5544 Fax: 44 (0) 20 7017 5198
Email: tf.enquiries@tfinforma.com

Taylor & Francis Inc, 325 Chestnut Street, Philadelphia, PA 19106, USA
Tel: +1 800 354 1420 (toll-free calls from within the US)
or +1 215 625 8900 (calls from overseas) Fax: +1 215 625 2940
Email: customerservice@taylorandfrancis.com

View an online sample issue at:
www.informaworld.com/rpop

Routledge
Taylor & Francis Group

Patterns of Prejudice

EDITORS:

David Cesarani, *Royal Holloway, University of London, UK*
Tony Kushner, *University of Southampton, UK*
Barbara Rosenbaum, *University of Southampton, UK*

Patterns of Prejudice *Patterns of Prejudice* provides a forum for exploring the historical
roots and contemporary varieties of social exclusion and the
demonization or stigmatisation of the Other. It probes the language
and construction of 'race', nation, colour, and ethnicity, as well as
the linkages between these categories. It encourages discussion
of issues at the top of the public policy agenda, such as asylum,
immigration, hate crimes and citizenship. As none of these issues
are confined to any one region, *Patterns of Prejudice* maintains
a global optic, at the same time as scrutinizing intensely the history
and development of intolerance and chauvinism in the United States
and Europe, both East and West.

Patterns of Prejudice is a peer reviewed journal published five
times a year. The views expressed in its pages are those of the
individual authors. The editors welcome the submission of articles for publication in *Patterns of Prejudice*.
These should be between 4000 and 7000 words. In exceptional cases, longer articles will be considered.
All articles must be the original work of the author(s.)

For further information on the journal and to submit an article, please visit the journal's website at
www.tandf.co.uk/journals/rpop

2007 Impact Factor: 0.302
Rankings: 5/9 (Ethnic Studies)
© Thomson Reuters, Journal Citation Reports 2008.

To sign up for tables of contents, new publications and citation alerting services visit **www.informaworld.com/alerting**

eupdates
Taylor & Francis Group

Register your email address at **www.tandf.co.uk/journals/eupdates.asp** to receive information
on books, journals and other news within your areas of interest.

Powered by
informaworld

For further information, please contact Customer Services at either of the following:
T&F Informa UK Ltd, Sheepen Place, Colchester, Essex, CO3 3LP, UK
Tel: +44 (0) 20 7017 5544 Fax: +44 (0) 20 7017 5198
Email: subscriptions@tandf.co.uk
Taylor & Francis Inc, 325 Chestnut Street, Philadelphia, PA 19106, USA
Tel: +1 800 354 1420 (toll-free calls from within the US)
or +1 215 625 8900 (calls from overseas) Fax: +1 215 625 2940
Email: customerservice@taylorandfrancis.com

View an online sample issue at:
www.tandf.co.uk/journals/rpop

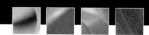

Journal of Intercultural Studies

EDITORS:
Dr Tseen Khoo, *Monash University, Australia*
Dr Vince Marotta, *Deakin University, Australia*

BOOK REVIEW EDITOR:
Dr Ajaya Sahoo, *University of Hyderabad, India*

ASSOCIATE EDITOR:
Paula Muraca, *Monash University, Australia*

Journal of Intercultural Studies showcases innovative scholarship about emerging cultural formations, intercultural negotiations and contemporary challenges to cultures and identities.

Journal of Intercultural Studies welcomes theoretically informed articles from diverse disciplines that contribute to the following discussions:

- Reconceptualising notions of nationhood, citizenship and racialisation;
- Questioning theories of diaspora, transnationalism, hybridity and 'border crossing' and their contextualised applications;
- Exploring the contemporary sociocultural formations of ethnicity, postcolonialism and indigeneity;
- Examining how past and contemporary key scholars can inform current thinking on cross-cultural knowledge, multiculturalism, race and cultural identity;

Journal of Intercultural Studies is an international, interdisciplinary journal that particularly encourages contributions from scholars in cultural studies, sociology, gender studies, political science, cultural geographers, urban studies, race and ethnic studies.

It is a peer-reviewed, critical scholarly publication that features articles, review essays and book reviews. Regular special issues provide stimulating, focused engagement with topical political, social and theoretical questions.

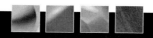